May 1993

To Jane,

I hope you enjoy our wine & food combina...

Good cooking

Kevin

Windows on the World

Wine and Food Book

Windows on the World

Wine and Food Book

Kevin Zraly
and
Hermann Reiner

 Sterling Publishing Co., Inc. New York

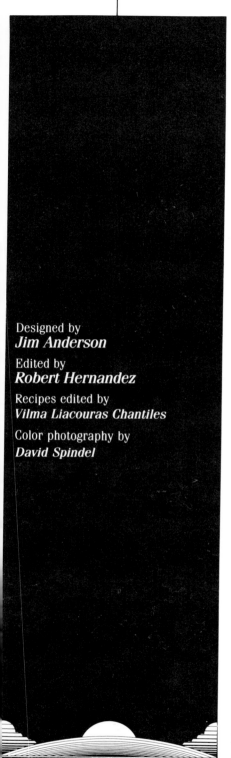

Designed by
Jim Anderson

Edited by
Robert Hernandez

Recipes edited by
Vilma Liacouras Chantiles

Color photography by
David Spindel

Acknowledgments

This book is dedicated to everyone who has dined at Windows on the World, the people responsible for making it a success, and the staff of Inhilco.

Very sincere thanks to Anton Aigner and Alan Lewis.

Food author Hermann Reiner would like to thank his brigade at Windows on the World; only with their help was it possible to compile these recipes: sous chefs Siegfried Hohaus and Karl Schmid and pastry chefs Michelle Tampakis and Peter Begusch. Thanks to editor Vilma Chantiles at Sterling. To my wife, Aurea, I express my deepest gratitude for her support and understanding during the long hours I worked all these years from the time I became the executive chef at Windows on the World.

Wine author Kevin Zraly would like to thank Felicia Sherbert for her writing contributions and ideas, Kathleen Talbert at Food and Wines from France for her help in writing the wine and cheese chapter, Robert Hernandez who edited the book and put it all together, Jim Anderson whose inventive design concepts made such a lively format, Burton Hobson who "suffered" through all of our wine and food tastings, Barry Mills and the wine department at Windows for their invaluable assistance, Philip Romeo for the menu script, and Lois Arrighi for her many hours preparing the manuscript.

Library of Congress Cataloging-in-Publication Data
Zraly, Kevin.
    Windows on the World wine and food book.

    Includes index.
    1. Cookery, International.   2. Wine and
wine making.   3. Windows on the World (New York, N.Y.)
I. Reiner, Hermann, 1948–   . II. Title.
TX725.A1Z73   1986   641.5′09   86-14685
ISBN 0-8069-4812-4

Copyright © 1986 by Inhilco, Inc.
Two Park Avenue, New York, N.Y. 10016
Distributed in Canada by Oak Tree Press Ltd.
% Canadian Manda Group, P.O. Box 920, Station U
Toronto, Ontario, Canada M8Z 5P9
Distributed in the United Kingdom by Blandford Press
Link House, West Street, Poole, Dorset BH15 1LL, England
Distributed in Australia by Capricorn Ltd.
P.O. Box 665, Lane Cove, NSW 2066
Manufactured in the United States of America

Contents

EQUIVALENTS
(Approximate Measurements)

Liquids

1 ounce = 2 tablespoons
   (6 teaspoons)
2 ounces = ¼ cup
8 ounces = 1 cup

Dry and Fresh Ingredients

Almonds (whole): 6 ounces = 1 cup
  (ground or slivered):
    4 ounces = ¾ cup
Blueberries (pint) = 14 ounces
Butter: 1 ounce = 2 tablespoons
Carrot (medium) = 6 ounces
Celery (stalk) = 2½ ounces
Chocolate: 1 ounce = 1 square
Fennel (bulb) = 8 ounces
Flour (all-purpose): 1 pound (loosely
    poured) = 3½ cups
  cake: 1 pound = 3¾ cups
Garlic (medium clove): ¹⁄₁₆ ounce or
  ¼ teaspoon
Leek = 7 ounces
Mushrooms (sliced or diced):
    8 ounces = 2½ cups
Onion (medium) = 4 ounces
  (sliced or diced):
    1 pound = 3½–4 cups
Pepper (green or red bell, medium)
  = 6 ounces
Potato (medium) = 4 ounces
  (diced): 1 pound = 3½–4 cups
Raspberries (½ pint) = 6½ ounces
Rice (raw, long-grained):
    1 pound = 2½ cups
Shallot: ¾ ounce = 1 tablespoon
Spinach leaves (10) = 4 ounces
Strawberries (1 pint) = 12 ounces
Sugar (granulated): 1 pound = 2 cups
  (powdered or confectioners'):
    1 pound = 4 cups
Tomato (medium) = 4 ounces
Tomatoes (chopped and drained):
    1 pound = 1½ cups
Tomato paste: 2 ounces = ¼ cup
Walnuts: 1 pound = 3½ cups

A Note on Equivalents

The recipes in this book, which I am pleased to share, come directly from our working files at Windows on the World. As in all professional kitchens (and, in fact, even in home kitchens in most countries except the United States), we work in weights (ounces and pounds) rather than by measuring with the traditional cups and tablespoons. We weigh all dry and fresh ingredients on our kitchen scale. In Europe and many countries, the metric system is used with grams and kilos in both shopping and cooking, making it simple for the home cook.

Whichever system you use, weighing is the most accurate and foolproof way of measuring ingredients. A cup of flour, for example, holds a different amount when it's packed tightly than when loosely filled. A cup of thinly sliced mushrooms will have a different weight, depending upon how you slice them. Moreover, having recipes in ounces greatly facilitates increasing them according to the size of your party.

Every serious cook has a food scale at home. More scales are being sold now than ever before, especially considering these diet-conscious days. If you don't have a kitchen scale, therefore, I urge you to buy one. The scale should be accurate to the half ounce and be capable of weighing up to five pounds. It should have a pan that you can fill with fresh or dry ingredients. I think you will soon prefer this handy and accurate procedure when cooking.

If you do not yet have a scale, use the Equivalents list at left, keeping in mind that the measurements are approximate. When the food is liquid, the ounces are by volume (32 ounces = 4 cups = 2 pints = 1 quart); when solid, the food ounces are by weight (16 ounces = 1 pound).

I believe your journey through this book will be full of interesting discoveries and pleasant experiences. Have fun cooking!

Hermann Reiner
Executive Chef

Foreword

While you will find many general principles for matching wine with food in our book, I have also suggested specific wines for many of the individual recipes. For the most part, I have recommended wines that are widely available, in addition to giving the reasons for the selections. Hopefully, you will find this useful in choosing wines from among your favorites. Many recommendations are based upon what our guests have enjoyed with these dishes at Windows on the World. I have also included some of my favorite wine and food combinations. These thoughts may provide you with a starting point for discovering the combinations that are most pleasing to you.

The recipes for our book were chosen to represent a broad range of the dishes served in our restaurants as well as for their harmonious accompaniment to fine wine. They vary from simple to a few at near-professional level, but even the most difficult can be successfully prepared in your kitchen with proper advance preparation. The secret is to read and reread the recipes until you have a clear understanding of the steps in their preparation. Throughout the book, I have added hints and comments to guide you in planning delectable wine and food menus.

We wish you all the best in preparing the recipes and choosing the right wines to complement them. Feel free to write us about your experiences. *Bon appétit* and *santé*!

Windows on the World
One World Trade Center
New York, NY 10048
Kevin Zraly (106th Floor)
Hermann Reiner (107th Floor)

Preface

Windows on the World is the ensemble of restaurants a quarter mile high atop New York's World Trade Center. It is the most spectacular dining complex in the world. Its ambience is New York elegant and it provides a breathtaking 55-mile view of bridges, skyscrapers, and harbor. It has the largest sales volume of any restaurant facility in the United States and its restaurants and six separate kitchens occupy a full acre of space.

Windows on the World was founded on the proposition that there is no great meal without great wine. Windows on the World stores 60,000 bottles in its on-premises cellar and warehouse, and every item on the menu is created to be complemented with appropriate wines.

The Restaurant is the main dining room. Its menu is international, to appeal to today's more widely travelled and knowledgeable guest. The Restaurant offers more than 100 wines on its regular list, and a cellarmaster's special selection offers 600 or more different wines at any given time.

Between noon and three o'clock on weekdays, Windows on the World becomes the Club, a private luncheon club for many of the executives who work in the World Trade Center and the surrounding financial district. Stored in a special wine cellar are the members' favorite wines, which they can purchase for a fraction above cost.

The Cellar in the Sky is the jewel of Windows on the World, renowned for its epicurean marriages of wine and food. Six evenings a week, just 36 guests are seated for a special seven-course dinner with five accompanying wines. The menu is changed every two weeks. The chef prepares creative new recipes or innovative presentations of classic dishes; the cellarmaster selects the proper wines to complement the courses or challenges the chef to prepare a dish that will be a perfect accompaniment to a specific wine.

The Hors D'Oeuvrerie features small-portion delicacies from around the world along with cocktails or any wine from the list. Regular events concentrate on specific regional foods and native chefs are flown in to prepare them authentically. The City Lights Bar is located in the middle of the network of dining rooms and stocks 1,000 brands of liquor, making drink choices limitless.

The staff at Windows on the World is fully and carefully trained in both wine and food service. The Wine School, which is now open to the public, began as a staff training program for everyone involved in wine service.

Windows on the World is directed by Alan Lewis and managed by Inhilco, a wholly owned subsidiary of Hilton International. Inhilco and its president Anton Aigner also operate 27 other food-service units at the World Trade Center. These units range in style from the Coffee Express, for commuters, to the Market Dining Room, a softly lit and elegantly appointed restaurant serving fresh seafood and steaks to those who prefer leisurely dining. These separate facilities serve not only to create a variety of dining experiences, but also permit the individual managers to meet customers as they would at a smaller establishment.

The basic concept created when Windows on the World first opened its doors in 1976 remains unchanged—the ultimate harmony of food and wine. It is an idea that is completely compatible with our times. And, as far as we can tell, like our wines, it can only improve with age.

9

Prelude to Wine & Food

When it comes to making a wine selection, many people still rely on the ever-faithful rule: "Red with meat, white with fish." That may have been fine years ago when everyone had a more "meat and potatoes" outlook on food. However, it leaves a lot to be desired for food and wine combinations today.

Twenty years ago, the average American adult ate in a restaurant for one of every six meals. Today we go out for one of every three meals. The biggest change, however, is our attitude towards food. Then people went out to *eat*, but today we go out to *dine*. Not only do we linger over gourmet meals, but our social evenings are often planned around dinner. As a result, wine has become a more important element in our dining experience, even though it still isn't part of the daily ritual in the United States as it is in Europe.

I'm still of the opinion that wine hasn't become an institution in the United States because of the mystery and confusion about it. It doesn't have to be that way. For the past ten years, Windows on the World has prided itself on making the wine and food experience full of pleasurable taste sensations for its guests, encouraging them to experiment with other wine and food combinations.

This is the premise for this book—to encourage you to experiment with wine and food. We try to answer the most frequently asked questions in the Wine School at Windows on the World and in the Restaurant. Whether you are an oenophile or a galloping gourmet at home, we try to give you enough knowledge to choose a wine with food, while not overwhelming you with the history of the grape. Hermann Reiner, the Restaurant's executive chef, gives you a glimpse into the kitchens of Windows on the World, complete with full menus, and easy-to-follow recipes. Color photos of some of his creations let you see if the masterpiece you prepare looks similar to his.

While we were writing this book, we tested Hermann's recipes, and we specially selected the wines to go with the menus. What makes the *Windows on the World Wine and Food Book* unique is that we do more than make particular wine recommendations. We tell you *why* we have made each choice. Then, if you wish, you can choose a substitute wine to go with any one of our menus because you will understand the logic that went into our selections.

Are there specific rules about matching wine and food?

There are no set rules to follow about matching your favorite cuisines and wines, but there are suggestions that we can make based on our experience of trying particular wines and foods for ourselves, as well as observing what our guests have at Windows on the World. Some of the most basic suggestions include having light wines with light meals, and more robust wines with hearty meals. If you are having more than one wine with a meal, start with the lightest and simplest, and work your way up to the more full-bodied wines. The reason is that you'll enjoy all of the wines if you follow the "natural progression," rather than allow a heavy wine to mask the flavor of a lighter one.

What makes a wine light, medium, or full bodied?

This is determined by the grapes used to make the wine, where the grapes are grown, the vintage, and the producer.

○ *Grapes*, of course, are vital to the whole process because the wine can only be as good as the grapes that make it. The grapes have distinct characteristics and flavors. Some of the more popular white grapes are Chardonnay, Sauvignon Blanc, and Riesling. Red grape favorites include Pinot Noir, Cabernet Sauvignon and Zinfandel.

○ *Where the grapes are grown* is important. White grapes, for instance, grow well in cool northern climates. The further north you go, the more acidity the white grapes will have, because there isn't as much sunshine to ripen the grapes. The Loire Valley, Alsace, Chablis, and Champagne regions of France are good examples of where white grapes grow best. On the other side, red grapes do much better in warm southern climates. Spain and Italy are countries famous for their robust red wines.

○ *Vintage* is no more than a weather report for the year. In a good vintage or year, there is a lot of sunshine that ripens the grapes and gives them plenty of sugar. Sweeter grapes produce a wine with a higher alcohol level, which occurs through fermentation. A high alcohol content often yields a wine with a full body.

Here is the formula for fermentation:
Sugar + Yeast = Alcohol + Carbon Dioxide (CO_2)

○ The *producer* of the wine gives you an idea of its quality before you even open the bottle. The producer may grow his own

Chardonnay grapes are the most expensive white grapes, which are grown primarily in the Burgundy and Champagne regions of France and in California. They make a full and fruity style of wine.

Sauvignon Blanc is grown primarily in the Loire Valley, the Graves and Sauternes regions of France, Washington State, and California. The white wine made from these grapes can be dry or sweet, and often herbal in flavor, depending on the location.

Riesling is a white grape grown in Alsace, Germany, and California, but it is most often associated with German wines.

Cabernet Sauvignon has become known as the classic red grape of California, which is responsible for some of the big red wines made there. Some of the best French Bordeaux wines are made from the same grape.

Pinot Noir is the red grape used to produce wines from Burgundy and Champagne, and it is also grown in California.

Zinfandel is another popular grape for red wine. However, today you are more likely to find the lighter version with the salmon-colored or orange hue called "blush" wine.

Fermentation is the process by which grape juice is made into wine.

Some well-known and reliable producers are Baron Patrick Ladoucette (Loire Valley); Louis Latour, Joseph Drouhin, Louis Jadot (Burgundy); Robert Mondavi, Louis Martini, Rodney Strong (California); Rudolf Müller (Germany); Paul Jaboulet (Côtes du Rhône); Bruno Prats (Bordeaux); Ruffino, Antinori (Italy); Torres (Spain); and there are many others.

Light-Bodied White Wines
Pinot Blanc (Alsace)
Riesling (Alsace)
Chablis (France)
Muscadet (Loire Valley)
Kabinett (Germany)
Orvieto (Italy)
*Sauvignon Blanc (California)
Riesling (California)
Soave (Italy)
Verdicchio (Italy)
Corvo (Italy)
Pinot Grigio (Italy)

grapes, buy grapes from other farmers in the region, or even do both. What's important is that the producer creates the style of wine by making it from his own recipe, the way a fine chef does in the kitchen. That's why you can have two bottles of Cabernet Sauvignon side by side that have a distinctly different flavor. Even though both wines are made from the same grape, they can taste as different as night and day. One wine may have been aged in oak barrels, whereas the other spent more time in stainless-steel tanks. These are just two possible variations on the recipe, which is determined entirely by the producer.

Here are lists to give you a better idea of the difference between light-, medium-, and full-bodied wines—both white and red. (Note: A single asterisk indicates that the style of wine can vary from light to heavy. A double asterisk pertains to French white Burgundy wines. The higher the quality and the better the vintage, the fuller the wine. For lists about the styles of Champagne, see page 67.)

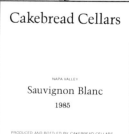

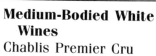

Medium-Bodied White Wines

Chablis Premier Cru (France)
Mâcon (Burgundy)
*Pouilly-Fumé (Loire Valley)
*Sancerre (Loire Valley)
*Sauvignon Blanc (California)
White Graves (Bordeaux)
Montagny (Burgundy)
St-Véran (Burgundy)

Full-Bodied White Wines

**Chablis Grand Cru (Burgundy)
Chardonnay (California)
**Chassagne-Montrachet (Burgundy)
**Puligny-Montrachet (Burgundy)
**Meursault (Burgundy)

Sweet White Wines

Auslese (Germany)
Beerenauslese (Germany)
Tröckenbeerenauslese (Germany)
Late-Harvest Riesling (California)
Sauternes (Bordeaux)
Beaumes-de-Venise (France)

Light-Bodied Red Wines

Bardolino
(Italy)
Beaujolais
(France)
Chianti
(Italy)
Rioja
(Spain)
Valpolicella
(Italy)

Medium-Bodied Red Wines

Beaujolais-Villages
(France)
Burgundy (French
regions, *i.e.*, Pommard,
Nuits-St-Georges,
Volnay)
*Cabernet Sauvignon
(California)
Chianti Classico
(Italy)
Côtes du Rhône
(France)
Dolcetto (Italy)
*Petit Château
Bordeaux
Pinot Noir
(California)
Merlot
(California)
Zinfandel
(California)

A *petit château* is a lesser-known château that produces good-quality wines at reasonable prices.

Where do I begin when choosing a wine with food?

The best place to begin is with your own taste buds. Do you prefer red, white, or perhaps a blush wine? Dry or sweet? For any wine and food combination to be good, it has to suit your individual taste.

Although you have a seemingly endless number of choices, you should be aware that there are some wine and food combinations that simply don't mix well. This is often the case if you choose a distinct or strong-tasting food like rack of lamb or Roquefort cheese. Try to have an ordinary table wine with either one and you'll probably be disappointed. You will only taste the lamb or the Roquefort because it will overpower the wine. The same is true if you decide to have a full-bodied wine, such as a red Rhône, with broiled chicken. You'll hardly taste the food.

Whether you're cooking a meal at home or ordering from a restaurant, which do you choose first—the wine or the food?

If you're putting together a seasonal menu—one that in- cludes soft shell crabs, or white asparagus, for example—or if you decide to have a special dish in a restaurant, let the food be your guide and select the wine to complement the food. On the other hand, if you are a wine aficionado and insist on serving a par- ticular wine or having it in a restaurant, by all means do so, but consider the style of the wine when you choose your food.

Full-Bodied Red Wines
Barbaresco (Italy)
Barolo (Italy)
Bordeaux (France)
Châteauneuf-du-Pape
 (France)
Grand Cru Burgundy
 (France)
Premier Cru Burgundy
 (France)
Hermitage (France)

If you're going to a restaurant, it's probably more natural for most people to choose the food first since that is the real reason for dining out. Actually, many styles of wine were created to go with particular foods. Look at the Muscadet region of France, for example. Muscadet is located near the water, and it's always been a fishing town—oysters and clams, mostly. The wine that comes from Muscadet is a dry white style, which happens to complement oysters and clams the best. In fact, it used to be common to see a paper oyster shell of some sort hanging around the top of the bottle of Muscadet.

The Man from Provence

One evening when I was working at Windows on the World, a gregarious-looking gentleman asked me to help him remember a very special wine that he had had before, but whose name he just couldn't remember.

"Let me describe it to you," he told me, "so you'll know the one that I'm talking about. I was in Provence last year on holiday with my mistress. We stayed in one of the finest hotels—on the 29th floor, overlooking the sea. One evening we had dinner on the veranda. The moon was shining, and it was just beautiful. We had a rosé wine from Provence, and it was the best wine I've ever tasted. Can you duplicate that for me?"

"Sir," I answered, "to be quite honest with you, I could probably duplicate the hotel, the service, the moonlight, and maybe even your mistress, but I could never duplicate the taste of the wine you describe from Provence."

For that afternoon barbecue, we suggest a basic Beaujolais. It's light and fruity, goes well with grilled or barbecued meats, and it's "non-cerebral," which means that you don't have to concentrate on its complexity. Just drink and enjoy!

Does the time of day have anything to do with the type of wine that should be served with a meal?

Absolutely, and it should suit the occasion as well. For example, you probably would not break out the '59 Lafite for an afternoon steak barbecue, but you may consider it for a special evening—perhaps a black tie event, when châteaubriand is the main fare. Without a doubt, ambiance is an important consideration in selecting wine.

Can you serve wines without food?

Certainly. Just make sure that the wine is not too heavy or tannic, because full-flavored wines are more suitable to serve with a meal. A light evenly balanced wine with a hint of fruit is the best one to drink when you're not eating food. Jug wines, Beaujolais, or German wines are good choices.

Would you serve different wines at different times of the year?

Once again, there's no rule dictating that you must have a certain wine at one time of the year and something else at another. However, people tend to drink more red wines in the winter because they are fuller and served at room temperature, while white wines have more refreshing thirst-quenching qualities that make them more popular in the summer.

What kind of wine should I have with Chinese food?

Personally, we agree with many food writers and would prefer to have beer with it. But if you have to make a choice, a sparkling wine would probably be best—perhaps an inexpensive Champagne. The carbonation cuts through the varied flavors of Chinese cooking, and it doesn't get lost by the strong flavors in that type of cuisine.

In many of the popular ethnic cuisines, the focus is on spiciness. When you have zesty foods, you can't help but become thirsty. If you try to drink only wine with some spicy cuisines (Cajun, Indian, Szechuan), you'll probably drink too much, trying to put out the fire in your mouth! That's why we sometimes suggest a cold, icy beer for these dishes—or water.

The Spice of Life

Strong-tasting, distinct flavors are characteristic of most ethnic cuisines. You can match a wine with practically any dish, but you should always consider the "active" ingredients in a dish, such as chili peppers in Tex-Mex dishes or curry in Indian dishes. Here is a list of some strong-tasting ingredients that can overpower a wine when used in excess:

- cilantro
- chili pepper
- cumin
- curry
- fennel
- garlic
- jalapeño peppers
- onions
- ginger
- paprika
- sage
- vinegar
- anchovy paste
- rosemary leaves

It's not unusual for a home gourmet to close the cookbook every so often and experiment with a combination of spices. Hermann has come up with a list of a few "no-nos" about spicing it up in the kitchen:

- thyme and rosemary
- thyme and sage
- tarragon and rosemary
- oregano and thyme
- paprika and sage
- paprika and rosemary

We've been talking a lot about flavors, but I have to reveal another little secret. It's very important to consider texture when choosing a wine.

"Do you still maintain that we're nothing but barbarians?"

1946

What do you mean by texture?

There is a difference in the texture between a steak or a chop, and a fillet of fish or a lobster tail. While the meat is more substantial and is more chewy, the fillet cuts easier and falls apart in your mouth, but the lobster tail has a firmness to it. You can take it a step further and look at the difference in texture of the cut of meat (sirloin steak versus filet mignon) or fish (fish steak versus fillet). Also consider the way you like to have food cooked—rare, medium, or well-done. This changes the texture and decidedly the flavor.

The point is that wine has a texture, just the way food does, and there are little nuances of flavor in a wine that can make it an adequate or unforgettable selection with the meal. A general rule of thumb, however, is that the sturdier or fuller in flavor the food is, the more full-bodied the wine should be.

Cooking with Wine

Wine is an important ingredient in the preparation of many foods. Its various uses include:

○ basic sauces ○ meat tenderizer ○ salad dressings
○ glazes   ○ marinades   ○ desserts

The way in which we use wine in the kitchen depends on its purpose and prominence in a particular dish. There is a significant difference in the preparation of Côte de Boeuf with Bordelaise Sauce versus spicing up a dish by adding a little wine. That's why we consider wine in the kitchen as a spice, which is meant to add flavor to the food.

Most restaurants—even the finest ones—use a reliable, inexpensive wine to cook with, which you may know as a jug wine. You are much better off using a jug wine than a cooking wine bought in a grocery store because the quality is much better. There's much less salt in a regular wine (a trace, if any), whereas cooking wine is loaded with sodium.

When we make basic stocks, it doesn't really matter what kind of wine is used because it evaporates. However, the wine is crucial to a sauce because you will definitely taste it; it doesn't boil away.

Is there such thing as a white wine that goes with steak and chops?

Certainly. The best thing to do is check back with the list of light-, medium-, and full-bodied wines. It is intended to be a reference guide. In this case, some California winemakers produce excellent full-bodied Chardonnays. Sonoma-Cutrer, Grgich Hills, and Edna Valley are just three California Chardonnays that go well with steak. There are several others. The French have been making full-bodied white wines for years, such as Chassagne-Montrachet and Meursault, which go perfectly with steak if you don't want to have a red Cabernet Sauvignon or a Rhône wine, for example.

Do sauces play a major role when you're choosing a wine?

Yes, because the sauce can change the whole taste of a dish, and the wine you have with it. The sauce transforms the dish into a new creation that can pass through any number of ethnic cuisines. You can take the same chicken breast and sauté it in garlic sauce, lemon sauce, with curry, mustard, or stuff it with bread crumbs. You certainly cannot choose the same wine to go with this vast assortment of dishes.

Even before people became more daring in experimenting with the new-style cuisines, they always seemed to order duck à l'orange with wild rice. This is probably one of the most difficult foods to match because of the sweet orange sauce. For this type of dish, we recommend a sparkling wine, preferably a Champagne. The carbonation cuts through the sweetness of the sauce and complements the dish nicely.

Are there any wine and food combinations that you consider "natural"?

Five combinations come to mind immediately, which go together as well as bread and butter. In terms of French wines, I would match the following foods:

○ Charcuterie—Alsace Riesling
○ Goat cheese—Sancerre
○ Oysters—Muscadet
○ Lamb—red Bordeaux
○ Roquefort cheese—Sauternes

Are there any problem foods when it comes to matching wines with them?

We don't like to think of them as problem foods, but as opportunities to try a new and different combination. These situations occur with asparagus, artichokes, anchovies, and pickled foods. In these cases, however, we look at the rest of the menu and pay careful attention to how the dish is prepared. Does the asparagus have Hollandaise sauce on it? Are the artichokes in a vinaigrette or stuffed Italian style? These are the considerations. If you are just sitting down to eat a jar of pickled okra, you are probably not too fussy about what to drink with it.

GRGICH HILLS

Napa Valley
CHARDONNAY
1984
PRODUCED AND BOTTLED BY
GRGICH HILLS CELLAR, RUTHERFORD, CA
ALCOHOL 13.4% BY VOLUME

Cooking with wine does not add calories. A dry table wine loses 85 percent of its calories when heat from cooking burns away the alcohol.

It is not always necessary to cook with the wine you will be drinking with dinner. An inexpensive wine basically adds the same flavor to the food as a premium one.

What if I'm giving a dinner party and I want to have both a red and a white wine for my guests?

If you're trying to please a crowd, you are very safe staying in the Beaujolais family for a red wine, and a basic white wine from the Mâconnais region of France. Both wines are easy to drink, represent a good value, and go well with many foods.

In a regular party situation in which you may have light hors d'oeuvres, plan on about ½ bottle per person. That's the equivalent of about two glasses. If you are having a dinner party where there is more food involved, to be on the safe side, plan on ¾ bottle per person. Always have plenty of water on hand for your guests to break up their wine drinking.

How many different wines can I serve with one meal?

You can serve one throughout the meal, if you wish, or you could serve a different wine with each course, as we do at the Cellar in the Sky. If you're serving one wine, just make sure that it's a well-balanced, easy-to-drink wine. This will make it more palatable to your guests. If you opt to serve more than one wine, try to match the individual courses to the wines, or vice versa, by using the logic that we discuss throughout the book.

Speaking of Body . . .

When I was the cellarmaster at Windows on the World, I was once called over to a woman's table to help her select a wine.

"What style of wine would you care for?" I asked.

"Oh, a full-bodied, dry white wine," she answered matter-of-factly.

"What type of wine do you usually have?" I inquired.

"Blue Nun," she replied.

For those of you who have never tried Blue Nun, it's a nice, easy-to-drink white wine, but it doesn't fit the description given by the woman in the restaurant that evening. It's all a matter of taste, and what tastes good to you.

Can you serve wine with dessert?

At the Cellar in the Sky, we serve the dessert wine a few minutes *before* the dessert actually arrives to prepare you for what's to come. But yes, you can serve a dessert wine with dessert. The most popular dessert wines are from Germany, the late-harvest Rieslings from California, as well as the Sauternes from France. They are all sweet and are meant to go with a dessert. The sweetness closes your palate and makes you feel satisfied after a good meal.

Can *you serve sparkling wines with dessert?*

If you are going to serve a sparkling wine with dessert, I recommend one with a little sweetness. Look for the words "demi-sec" on the label, which means the sparkling wine has a little sweetness to it. Avoid the extra-dry "brut" at the end of the meal, which has no sweetness at all.

The Ten Commandments of Wine and Food

1. Thou shalt not let others dictate thy taste. The definition of a good wine is one that tastes good to you.

2. Thou shalt not take out a second mortgage on thy home to enjoy a good bottle of wine.

3. Thou shalt not be limited by "golden rules" of wine and food, for they do not exist. There are only "suggestions."

4. Thou shalt enjoy light meals with light wines, and hearty meals with more robust wines.

5. Thou shalt consider the sauces that are served with food, for they dictate the way thou shalt choose thy wine.

6. Thou shalt follow the "natural progression" of wine and food during the course of a meal, progressing from light to heavy.

7. Thou shalt consider the way thou prepares a particular food (rare, medium, well done), for its texture will help thou make thy wine choice.

8. Thou shalt be more adventurous in sampling regional wines and cuisines. Thou shalt keep an open mind in this endeavor.

9. Thou shalt not overindulge. Consume thy wine and food in moderation. (Thou shalt not dull thy senses by overindulging.)

10. Thou shalt look for the freshest ingredients possible when preparing thy recipes.

1954

"Something in a nice white wine."

Drawing by Geo. Price; © 1954, 1982
The New Yorker Magazine, Inc.

The Cellar
in the Sky

To get to the Cellar in the Sky, you are whisked up to the 107th floor of the World Trade Center in an elevator that seems capable of supersonic flight. As its name implies, it is a wine cellar, but not like a dark, damp one with cobwebs in some old French château—quite the opposite, in fact. The Cellar in the Sky is an intimate room with polished oak tables and comfortable leather-strapped chairs. The atmosphere is romantic, with dimly reflected light on wine bottles lining the walls and a classical guitarist playing softly in the background.

No other restaurant in New York has a separate room reserved exclusively for a full wine and food menu. It provides the chef and his staff the opportunity to be most creative—and even a little daring—because they only have to prepare dinner for 36 people. The chef coordinates the menu with the cellarmaster, who then must get the approval of the director of Windows on the World.

There is one seating at the Cellar in the Sky every evening at seven-thirty, except Sunday. Upon arrival, the guests are offered an apéritif, which usually includes a choice of Champagne, Lillet, Fino Sherry, Kir, or a white Burgundy wine. After canapés are served, the seven-course meal commences, progressing at a leisurely pace from the lighter dishes to the more substantial, with four corresponding wines. It is truly an experience of taste sensation. And the best part is that there are no decisions to be made. The guests just sit back and enjoy.

The menu is prepared around the wines, which is the concept of the wine cellar. There are exceptions to the rule, however. For instance, the chef's suggestions for desserts are almost always followed without question, and the last wine and dessert are served separately. The reason is simple: Many guests choose to make the sweet wine dessert by itself.

The exceptionally skilled staff at the Cellar in the Sky is largely responsible for the nightly success of these memorable gatherings. A staff of four presides over the room to cater to the guests and to keep their wine glasses filled. These staff members are among the best at Windows on the World, constantly trained and tested to ensure their ability and knowledge in the finer points of service.

Looking back on the early days at the Cellar in the Sky, it's hard to believe that it didn't catch on immediately. Like many of the other unique dining concepts implemented at Windows on the World, the cellar was years ahead of its time. Today, one decade later, the Cellar in the Sky is always filled to capacity, sometimes requiring reservations weeks or months in advance.

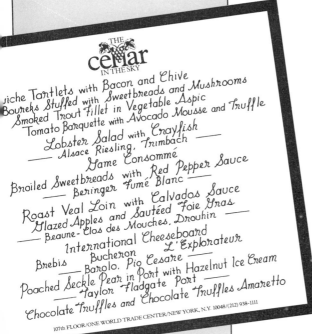

Quiche Tartlets with Bacon and Chive

Serves 8

for DOUGH

2¼ oz.	unsalted butter, cut in cubes
3½ oz.	all-purpose flour
	egg yolk
	salt

for FILLING

5 oz.	bacon
¼ oz.	chive, diced
2	eggs
4½ oz.	heavy cream
	salt
	white pepper, freshly ground
pinch	ground nutmeg

1 *To make the dough*: combine the butter, flour, egg yolk and salt in a bowl. Mix until the dough holds together. Wrap in plastic and refrigerate overnight.

2 When ready to use, roll the dough on a floured board till ⅛-inch thick. Cut into 2-inch rounds; press each round into individual 2-inch tartlet tins.

3 *To make the filling*: dice the bacon into ¼-inch pieces and sauté in a hot skillet until very crisp. Drain off the excess fat. Reserve the crisp bacon.

4 In a bowl, mix the eggs and cream. Add the seasonings and chive.

5 Divide the crisp bacon among the tartlet tins and fill with the custard.

6 Bake in a preheated oven at 325°F for about 15 minutes, avoiding top heat. Serve hot.

Boureks Stuffed with Sweetbreads and Mushrooms

Yields 12 triangles

8 oz.	sweetbreads	4 oz.	heavy cream
1 pt.	White Veal Stock (page 31)	2 oz.	Brown Veal Stock (page 153)
2 oz.	unsalted butter	1	parsley sprig, chopped
¼ oz.	shallot, chopped	1	chervil sprig, chopped
2 oz.	pleurottes or regular mushrooms, diced	2 pkgs.	strudel dough sheets or substitute filo (phyllo)
1 oz.	Madeira		
	salt	1 oz.	unsalted butter, melted, to brush on strudel
	white pepper, freshly ground		

1 Soak the sweetbreads in cold water for 1 hour to refresh; drain.

2 Poach sweetbreads in the White Veal Stock for 5 minutes; let cool in the stock.

3 When cool, remove sweetbreads and trim off the excess skin; cut sweetbreads into ¼-inch dice. You can save the stock for a soup or a sauce.

4 Heat a skillet and melt the 2 oz. of butter; add the shallot and mushrooms and sauté for half a minute.

5 Deglaze with the Madeira.

6 Add the sweetbreads and season with salt and pepper. Stir in the heavy cream and Brown Veal Stock. Reduce the liquid over high heat.

7 Add the parsley and chervil and set aside to cool. Correct the seasoning.

8 *To stuff the boureks*: Cut strudel dough sheets or filo lengthwise into 2-inch strips. On a clean surface, work with 1 strip at a time. Brush with melted butter. Place a teaspoon of filling on each strip and roll into triangles.

9 Arrange boureks on a greased baking sheet.

10 Bake in a preheated oven at 350°F until golden brown. Serve hot.

To make the boureks, we use Hungarian strudel dough sheets of 17″ × 23″ with four sheets to a package. You can substitute filo (fillo, phyllo) leaves, which are usually 14″ × 18″ with 20–22 leaves per package. Whichever you use, be sure to keep them covered to avoid drying out as you work. Cut the sheets in a stack, if you must cut them to a specific size, before buttering them.

At Windows on the World, we use the bounty of Mother Nature. Our wild mushrooms come primarily from the states of Washington, Oregon, and California. Chanterelles are available from July to December, *pied de moutons* from September to December, morels from April to December, and lobster mushrooms from September to November. Depending on the season, you can also use trumpets, hatch hogs, chicken of the woods or oyster mushrooms, or pleurottes.

Cèpes or stone mushrooms, considered delicacies, are called "the king of mushrooms." Very strong in flavor, cèpes can be added raw to salads or risotto, cooked in sauces or in terrines, pâtés, or galantines. They are found from July to November. Plain, cultivated mushrooms (champignons) are the most versatile vegetables, popular for salads and appetizers. They can be fried, broiled, sautéed or grilled, as well as chopped, sliced, or used whole to enhance the flavor of soups, sauces, and purées. Mushrooms are used with white and dark meats, poultry, and fish, and tossed into omelets, stuffings, and quiche.

Smoked Trout Fillet in Vegetable Aspic

Yields 12 slices (1 small terrine)

2 oz.	spinach leaves		1/8 oz.	white vinegar
2½ oz.	leek, diced			salt, as needed
2½ oz.	carrot, diced			white pepper,
2½ oz.	celery, diced			freshly ground
1	smoked trout fillet			Sherry Vinaigrette
5	gelatin leaves			(recipe follows)

1   In boiling salted water, blanch the washed spinach for a few seconds. Refresh the spinach in cold water; drain and squeeze dry.

2   Line the bottom of a small terrine with the spinach leaves, reserving some for the top.

3   Dice the leek, carrot, and celery. Blanch the diced vegetables; strain. Save the vegetable stock and reduce to about 5 oz.

4   Skin and clean the trout fillet.

5   Soak the gelatin in cold water until soft. Add to the hot vegetable stock with the vinegar to make the aspic; adjust the seasonings.

6   Spread a layer of diced vegetables over the spinach leaves in the terrine; then add the trout fillet and another layer of diced vegetables.

7   Fill the terrine with the vegetable aspic; cover with the remaining spinach leaves.

8   Refrigerate for at least 6 hours.

9   Slice carefully, dress on plate and serve with a sherry vinaigrette. Serve cold.

Tomato Barquette with Avocado Mousse and Truffle

Serves 12

3	large ripe tomatoes			freshly ground
1	ripe avocado		5 oz.	heavy cream
½	lemon, squeezed		2	frisée lettuce leaves
	for the juice			(curly-leaf endive)
	salt		1	small truffle, cut in
	white pepper,			julienne strips

Gelatin leaves are available in specialty shops. You may substitute unflavored gelatin and use a half package (1¼ oz.) for the 5 gelatin leaves in the recipe. To help you convert from gelatin leaves to granulated unflavored gelatin: Use 16 leaves to make a quart of gelatin; 8 leaves for 2 cups; 4 leaves for 1 cup.

Sherry Vinaigrette

3 oz.	olive oil
2 oz.	vegetable oil
1½ oz.	sherry vinegar
¼ oz.	chive, finely cut
¼ oz.	flat-leaf parsley, chopped
½ oz.	shallot, chopped
½ oz.	red bell pepper, finely diced
	salt to taste
	white pepper, freshly ground

1   Mix all the ingredients in a bowl or jar.

2   Let stand at room temperature for 30 minutes for flavor to fully develop.

3   Correct the seasoning.

A colorful garnish in which a tomato-wedge barquette is filled with a delicious cargo of avocado mousse.

1   Dip tomatoes in boiling water for 10 seconds. Rinse in cold water. Peel tomatoes and cut into sixths; remove the seeds.

2   Peel the avocado and mash it through a sieve. Mix the purée with the lemon juice, salt, and pepper.

3   Whip the heavy cream; fold in the avocado purée. Arrange a slice of lettuce on each tomato wedge.

4   Using a pastry bag, pipe avocado purée onto each wedge.

5   Garnish with a julienne slice of truffle. Serve cold.

Lobster Salad with Crayfish
Fresh Noodles, Fennel Purée, and Leek Rolls

Serves 8

	Fresh Noodles (recipe follows)
	Court Bouillon (recipe follows)
	Fennel Purée (recipe follows)
	Leek Rolls (recipe follows)
2 lbs.	*live crayfish*
4 (1¼ lbs. each)	*live lobsters*
10 oz.	*Warm Vinaigrette (recipe follows)*
6 oz.	*Sherry Vinaigrette (page 26)*
24	*fresh basil leaves*

1   After making the noodles, bouillon, and garnishes, clean the crayfish. Remove the intestines. Poach crayfish in the Court Bouillon for about 2 minutes. Remove crayfish from the liquid and set aside.

2   Poach the lobsters in the same liquid for about 15 minutes. Let cool in the liquid.

3   Break off and clean the crayfish tails. Break off and clean the lobster tails and claws. Cut the tails into nice medallions. Marinate in the Warm Vinaigrette.

4   Mix cooked, hot noodles with the cleaned crayfish tails and Sherry Vinaigrette.

5   *To serve*: Place noodles in the middle of the plate. Arrange the lobster medallions around the noodles; roll the leeks and place between each medallion. Spoon on the fennel purée near the leek rolls. Garnish each plate with 3 basil leaves. Serve warm. (Color photo on page A.)

Riesling, Trimbach—Alsace, France
People often think of Rieslings as sweet wines. All Alsace Rieslings, however, are totally dry, light in body, and because of the northern location of Alsace, have higher acidity. The acidity brings out the taste of Lobster Salad with Crayfish, making it a perfect accompaniment to this food. Trimbach is the producer of the Alsace Riesling chosen for this menu and the best recent vintages are 1983 and 1985.

Preparing the lobster and crayfish and assembling this delectable dish (pictured on the front cover) won't take too long, but you should have the noodles, court bouillon and garnishes ready first.

(continued)

Leek Rolls

3 young leeks
½ oz. shallot
½ oz. chive
3 oz. Sherry Vinaigrette
salt
white pepper, freshly
ground

1 Cut leeks in half lengthwise and rinse under running water; loosen the leeks so that they are completely separated. Cut off about 6 inches of each white end. (Use the green ends for the Court Bouillon).

2 Cook leeks in salted water for about 2 minutes and, while still hot, drop into the Sherry Vinaigrette to marinate. Keep warm.

3 Just before serving, roll up each leek. Arrange the rolls upright.

Court Bouillon

Yields 2 quarts

2 qts. water
16 oz. dry white wine
2 oz. celery, diced
3 oz. onion, diced
2 oz. carrot, diced
3 oz. leek, washed and diced
a few dill stems
a few parsley stems
1 bay leaf
5 white peppercorns
1 fresh thyme sprig
salt

1 Mix all the ingredients in a large saucepan.

2 Bring to a boil, lower the heat, and simmer for about 30 minutes. Strain and cool.

3 Refrigerate and use within 2 to 3 days; or freeze in small containers to use within 3 months.

FRESH NOODLES

Serves 8

8 oz. all-purpose flour
8 oz. durum wheat semolina
2 eggs
2 egg yolks
1 oz. olive oil
salt
lukewarm water, as needed
1 oz. vegetable oil

1 In a bowl; mix the flour, semolina, eggs, yolks, oil, salt, and enough water to make a firm dough.

2 Remove the dough from the bowl and knead on a wooden board for about 2 to 3 minutes until dough is smooth.

3 Dust with flour and let the dough rest for about 1 hour.

4 Roll out the dough as thinly as possible; cut into strips of the desired size.

5 In a pot, bring salted water to a boil and add the oil. Stir in the noodles and boil for about 1 to 2 minutes until they are still quite firm (al dente).

6 Drain; do not rinse.

FENNEL PURÉE

1 fennel head
½ lemon, squeezed for the juice
1 oz. shallot, chopped
2 oz. unsalted butter
2 oz. black cured olives, pitted
salt
white pepper, freshly ground

1 Cut fennel in half and loosen the ribs. Cut off the middle stalk.

2 Scrap the outer ribs, if necessary. Cook in salted water with a little lemon juice until tender. Chop the fennel.

3 Sauté the shallot in butter and add the fennel; then purée in a processor until smooth. Mash the purée through a fine strainer.

4 Chop and blanch the olives; drain and mix with the fennel. Season with salt and pepper.

5 Use a teaspoon of the mixture to form quenelle shapes when serving the salad.

WARM VINAIGRETTE

Yields 10 ounces

6 oz.	Lobster Stock (page 39)
1½ oz.	olive oil
1½ oz.	vegetable oil
1 oz.	sherry vinegar
¼ oz.	shallot, chopped
1	fresh basil sprig, chopped
	salt
	white pepper, freshly ground

1 Heat the stock almost to the boiling point.

2 In a blender, on low speed, mix hot stock with the oils, vinegar, shallot, salt and pepper.

3 Remove from the blender and pour into a bowl. Sprinkle in the chopped basil. Correct seasonings.

4 Place the warm lobster medallion into the dressing or pour the dressing on top.

Game Consommé

Serves 8 to 10

8 oz.	lean game meat
½ oz.	mushroom stems
1 oz.	celery
1 oz.	shallot
2	egg whites
1	bay leaf
3	juniper berries, crushed
5	white peppercorns, crushed
2 qts.	White Game Stock (recipe follows)
	salt, as needed
dash	fresh thyme
½ oz.	fresh chive, thinly sliced

1 Grind the game meat with the mushrooms, celery, and shallot through the coarse blade of a meat grinder.

2 Mix with the egg whites and some crushed ice. Add the bay leaf, juniper berries, and peppercorns; let rest for about 30 minutes.

3 Place mixture in a large pot and stir in the game stock, mixing carefully.

4 Over medium heat, bring to a boil, stirring occasionally on the bottom of the pot. Simmer gently for about 30 to 40 minutes. Season with salt to taste.

5 Strain through a cheesecloth. Degrease completely.

6 Sprinkle with the thyme and chive.

White Game Stock

Use quail, pheasant, wild duck, venison, or roebuck for this stock.

Yields 2 quarts

2 oz.	olive oil
3 lbs.	game bones, wings, necks, and trimmings
4 qts.	cold water
2 oz.	onion, diced
3 oz.	carrot, diced
3 oz.	leek, cut in half lengthwise
3 oz.	celery, diced
2 oz.	mushroom stems
1	fresh thyme sprig
1	fresh parsley sprig
1	fresh rosemary sprig
5	juniper berries
1	bay leaf
6	white peppercorns
¼ oz.	salt

1 In a heavy skillet or roasting pan, heat the olive oil; then add the bones and trimmings. Sauté lightly over medium heat.

2 Transfer the bones and trimmings to a stock pot and cover with the water. Bring to the boiling point. Degrease the liquid and skim off the foam.

3 Simmer for about 30 minutes and degrease again.

4 Add all the vegetables, spices, and herbs. Simmer for 30 minutes longer, adding water, if necessary.

5 Strain through cheesecloth into a saucepan.

6 Simmer over low heat until reduced to 2 quarts; let cool.

7 Keep in the refrigerator to use within 3 to 4 days; or store in small plastic containers in the freezer.

Beringer

Fumé Blanc
Dry Sauvignon Blanc

PRODUCED AND BOTTLED BY
BERINGER VINEYARDS, ST HELENA, NAPA VALLEY, CALIFORNIA
ALCOHOL 12.7% BY VOLUME

Beringer Fumé Blanc—Napa Valley, California

This Fumé Blanc is made from 100 percent Sauvignon Blanc grapes. The wine's medium body and balanced acidity go well with the texture of Broiled Sweetbreads with Red Pepper Sauce. A Chardonnay wine might be too strong for the sweetbreads, especially with this sauce.

You could prepare the sweetbreads a day in advance, as indicated in steps 2 and 3. The Red Pepper Sauce can also be made earlier and reheated. The celery leaves can be fried and red and green pepper garnish quickly sautéed before serving, just before broiling the sweetbreads.

Broiled Sweetbreads with Red Pepper Sauce
Fried Celery Leaves, and Red and Green Pepper Garnish

Serves 8

	Red Pepper Sauce (recipe follows)
	Fried Celery Leaves (recipe follows)
	Red and Green Pepper Garnish (recipe follows)
2 lbs.	sweetbreads, trimmed and skinned
16 oz.	White Veal Stock (recipe follows)
	salt
	white pepper, freshly ground
3 oz.	vegetable oil
½	lemon, squeezed for the juice

1 Prepare the sauce and garnishes.

2 Clean the sweetbreads, rinse in running water and soak for half an hour.

3 Heat the stock; add the sweetbreads and simmer for about 3 minutes. Remove from the heat and cool. (This much can be done a day in advance.)

4 Remove the cold sweetbreads from the stock and cut into ½-inch slices. Season with salt and pepper; dip in the oil.

5 Grill in a broiler or on a grill for about 3 minutes.

6 *To serve;* Ladle sauce on the middle of the heated plates. Arrange the sweetbreads and the celery and pepper garnishes nicely on each plate. Serve immediately. (Color photo on page B.)

RED PEPPER SAUCE

1 lb.	red bell pepper
3 oz.	shallot
2 oz.	unsalted butter
2 oz.	dry white wine
6 oz.	White Veal Stock (page 31)
8 oz.	heavy cream
½	lemon, squeezed for the juice
	salt to taste
	white pepper, freshly ground

1 Wash the red pepper, remove the stems and seeds; dice the peppers. Chop the shallot.

2 In a saucepan, sauté the red pepper and shallot in the butter. Deglaze with the wine. Add stock and simmer for about 10 minutes.

3 Stir in the cream. Simmer and reduce for a few minutes longer; then mix in a blender. Season with lemon juice, salt, and pepper. Strain through a fine Chinese strainer.

4 Keep warm until serving time.

WHITE VEAL STOCK

Yields 2 quarts

3½ lbs.	veal bones from loin, rack, or neck, and trimmings, cut into 1-inch pieces
4 qts.	cold water
8 oz.	onion, chopped
6 oz.	leek, washed and chopped
6 oz.	carrot, chopped
4 oz.	celery root, chopped
2 oz.	fresh mushroom stems or small mushrooms
1	fresh parsley sprig
1	fresh rosemary sprig
2	bay leaves
15	white peppercorns
½ oz.	salt

1 Wash veal bones in warm water to remove the blood.

2 Place bones in a large stockpot, add the water, and very slowly bring to a boil, skimming and discarding fat and foam as they rise to the surface. Simmer gently for 1 hour.

3 Add the vegetables, herbs, and spices and continue simmering for 30 minutes.

4 Set a Chinese strainer over a large saucepan and strain the stock. Skim off all the fat.

5 Place the saucepan over a low burner and slowly reduce to 2 quarts. Cool.

6 Refrigerate and use within 3 to 5 days; or freeze in 2-cup quantities for up to 3 months.

Fried Celery Leaves

3 oz. celery leaves
5 oz. vegetable oil
salt

1 Deep-fry the celery leaves in hot oil for about 3 seconds. Using a skimmer, immediately remove the leaves and set on a paper towel to dry. Dash with salt. Keep warm till ready to serve.

Red and Green Pepper Garnish

2 oz. unsalted butter
3 oz. green bell pepper, cut into fine strips
3 oz. red bell pepper, cut into fine strips
3 oz. celery, thinly sliced
salt
white pepper, freshly ground

1 Heat the butter in a skillet. Add the pepper and celery and sauté slightly. The vegetables should have a nice crunch. Season with salt and pepper.

Use this White Veal Stock for white cream sauces, mushroom sauces, cream soups, veal fricassee, dishes with sweetbreads, and other specialties.

Beaune, Clos des Mouches, Drouhin—Burgundy, France
This medium-bodied red wine is made from 100 percent Pinot Noir grapes and is produced by Joseph Drouhin. The red wines of Beaune are lighter in style than their counterpart from the Côte de Nuits. I chose a Burgundy wine to go with Roast Veal Loin with Calvados Sauce rather than a Bordeaux or a California Cabernet, which might have overpowered the meat with the foie gras. Look for the outstanding 1983 vintage.

Glazed Apples

2 Granny Smith apples
3 oz. unsalted butter
2 oz. sugar
2 oz. Calvados or applejack

1 Peel and core the apples; then cut into wedges

2 Heat the butter in a flat skillet, slip the apple wedges into the butter, and dash them with sugar. When browned on one side, turn the wedges and again dash with sugar. Sauté apples only until partially soft. Pour Calvados over the apples in the skillet, and flambé.

3 Set aside and keep warm.

Roast Veal Loin with Calvados Sauce
Glazed Apples, Sautéed Foie Gras and Celeriac, and Parsley Mousse

Serves 8

Calvados Sauce (recipe follows)
Glazed Apples (recipe follows)
Sautéed Foie Gras and Celeriac (recipe follows)
Parsley Mousse (recipe follows)
½ loin of veal (about 2½ lbs.)
2 oz. vegetable oil
salt to taste
white pepper, freshly ground

1 After making the garnishes, prepare the veal. Bone the veal loin and trim completely of any skin or fat. (Use the bone and trimmings to make any veal stock).

2 Season the veal on both sides. On a burner top, heat the oil in a roasting pan. Brown all surfaces of the veal. Place in a preheated oven, and roast at 375°F for about 12 minutes or until the meat is pink and elastic when you touch the meat with your fingers.

3 Let the meat rest for about 12 to 15 minutes before slicing; keep warm.

4 *To serve*: Arrange all ingredients on heated plates, starting with the sauce. Then place a slice of the veal loin over the sauce. Grind white pepper on top of the veal and foie gras. Garnish the plate with foie gras and celeriac and the parsley mousse. Serve warm.

Lobster Salad with Crayfish

Roast Veal Loin
with
Calvados Sauce

Broiled Sweetbreads
with Red Pepper Sauce

B

Salad of
Mallard Breast
with Asparagus

Poached Seckel Pear in Port

Lobster
Ravioli

C

American Venison,
Two Ways

Sautéed
Hudson Valley
Duck Liver
with
Truffles

D

E

Scallop of Salmon
with
Soy Beurre Blanc
and
Azuki Sprouts

Côte de Boeuf
and
Vegetable
Charlotte
with
Bordelaise Sauce

F

Baked Red Snapper with Confit of Vegetables

G

Feuillette of Mixed Berries

Orange Tart
with
Bitter Chocolate
Sorbet

Apple Charlotte

CALVADOS SAUCE

1	Granny Smith apple, peeled, cored, and diced
2 oz.	unsalted butter
2 oz.	Calvados or applejack
16 oz.	Brown Veal Stock (page 153)
10 oz.	heavy cream
2 oz.	unsalted butter, chilled
	salt
	white pepper, freshly ground

1 Sauté the apples in butter. Deglaze with the Calvados, and flambé.

2 Stir in the veal stock and simmer for 2 minutes; then add the heavy cream. Continue cooking for about 12 minutes.

3 Pour into a blender and whip until the sauce is smooth.

4 Add the chilled butter to the sauce. Season with salt and pepper.

5 Keep warm until needed.

PARSLEY MOUSSE   Serves 8

12 oz.	curly parsley
3 oz.	flat-leaf parsley
3 oz.	spinach leaves
1½ oz.	shallot, chopped
1 oz.	unsalted butter
6 oz.	crème double (12 oz. heavy cream reduced to half)
4 oz.	Crème Fraîche (page 36)
	salt
	white pepper, freshly ground
	ground nutmeg

1 Remove all the stems and thoroughly wash the parsley and spinach.

2 Bring salted water to a boil in a saucepan; blanch the spinach and the parsley for about 10 seconds. Immediately refresh the spinach and parsley under cold water. Drain and squeeze out all the water. Coarsely chop the spinach and parsley.

3 In a casserole, sauté the shallot in butter. Add the *crème double* and simmer until reduced; then add the chopped spinach and parsley. Cook for about 1 minute.

4 Purée through a sieve or in a food processor. Return the purée to the casserole and bring to a boil; season with salt, pepper, and nutmeg. Add crème fraîche.

5 When serving, shape with a soup spoon and dress directly on the plate. Serve warm.

Sautéed Foie Gras and Celeriac

12 oz.	fresh foie gras (duck liver)
1	celeriac
¼	lemon, squeezed
2 oz.	clarified unsalted butter
	salt
	white pepper

1 Cut the foie gras into 2 oz., ¼-inch-thick medallions; season with salt and pepper; set aside until Step 5.

2 Peel and slice the celery into ⅛-inch-thin slices. Using a round cookie cutter, cut into 1-½-inch-diameter circles.

3 Cook the celery in lightly salted water, acidulated with some lemon juice, until crisp. Refresh with cold water; dry the celery on a paper towel.

4 Sauté celery in the butter. Set aside and keep warm.

5 When all other garnishes and the veal are prepared, in a very hot skillet, sauté the foie gras in butter, until just pink inside.

Barolo, Pio Cesare—Piedmont, Italy
The "biggest" wine on this menu is the Barolo, produced by Pio Cesare and considered the king of Italian red wines. Since the Barolo is high in alcohol and tannin when young, it sometimes will overpower food, but in this case its tannin will be softened by the style of the cheeses that were matched with it. Pio Cesare recommends the 1971, 1978, and 1982 vintages. This menu is a good example of our Cellar in the Sky concept: progressing from light-style wine to a full-bodied one.

Taylor Fladgate Port— Oporto, Portugal
We frequently serve Port at the Cellar in the Sky during the colder months of the year. It is a fortified sweet wine with an alcohol content that sometimes approaches 21 percent. It is exactly the same red wine used in preparing the Poached Seckel Pear so it is a match that I guarantee will work. I recommend the 1963, 1966, 1970, and 1977 vintages.

Poached Seckel Pear in Port with Hazelnut Ice Cream

Serves 8

16	Seckel pears
1 bottle	port or dry red wine
8 oz.	sugar
1	lemon rind
1 oz.	cornstarch
1 recipe	Hazelnut Ice Cream (recipe follows)
8	Hippen Shells (page 35)

1 Peel the pears; in a medium saucepan, combine pears and three-fourths of the port, the sugar, and lemon rind.

2 Bring to a boil and reduce the heat; simmer for 5 to 6 minutes or until tender. Transfer pears to a dish.

3 Dissolve the cornstarch in the remaining port; stir into the hot port and pears. Boil 1 to 2 minutes until the sauce thickens.

4 Place 2 pears on each plate; pour a little sauce around them.

5 Fill each hippen shell with a scoop of ice cream and arrange on the plates with the pears. Serve chilled. (Color photo on page C.)

HAZELNUT ICE CREAM

Serves 8–10

16 oz.	heavy cream
7	egg yolks
6½ oz.	sugar
4 oz.	hazelnut paste (available in specialty shops) or
5 oz.	hazelnuts, toasted and ground

1 Bring the cream to a boil in a saucepan.

2 In a bowl, thoroughly mix the egg yolks with the sugar.

3 Add some of the boiling cream to the yolks. Then pour this mixture into the cream and heat to about 180°F. Stir in the hazelnut paste or the ground hazelnuts.

4 Remove from the burner and let cool, stirring occasionally.

5 Pour the mixture into an ice-cream or sherbet machine; freeze, according to manufacturer's instructions.

6 When frozen, put the ice cream into a plastic container; cover with plastic and store in the freezer.

HIPPEN SHELLS

3½ oz.	all-purpose flour	1¼ oz.	heavy cream	
3½ oz.	powdered sugar	1 oz.	unsalted butter, softened	
3½ oz.	milk	½ oz.	all-purpose flour	

1 In a bowl, combine the 3½ oz. of flour, powdered sugar, milk, and cream; mix with an electric mixer until smooth.

2 Smear the softened butter on a sheet pan and sprinkle with ½ oz. of flour. Drop the batter from a teaspoon several inches apart on the pan. Spread the batter with the back of spoon to make 2½-inch discs.

3 Bake at 320°F until golden brown.

4 While still hot, fold the discs over inverted espresso or mocha cups so that they will form shells. Cool the pastry on the cups; carefully remove. Store in covered containers or a freezer.

These pastry shells, called hippen in Austria and Germany, derive from the word that means hollow. The dough is baked like pancakes and, while still hot, rolled into hollow shells. We like to shape the hot pancakes over inverted cups to make shells. When cool, you can serve ice cream, sorbet, berries, and fruit sauces in them for a tasty and attractive dessert.

Chocolate Truffles **Yields 20 Truffles**

8 oz.	heavy cream	½ oz.	Grand Marnier, Kahlua,
1 oz.	unsalted butter		Fra Angelico, or
3 oz.	sugar		other liqueur
8 oz.	semisweet chocolate, melted	10 oz.	semisweet chocolate for coating

1 Bring cream, butter, and sugar to a boil in a saucepan. Remove from heat.

2 Melt the 8 oz. of semisweet chocolate on top of a double boiler over hot, not boiling, water, stirring occasionally.

3 Fold melted chocolate and Grand Marnier into the cream mixture. Chill until mixture just hardens, stirring from time to time. Mix with a spoon, just until the color lightens.

4 Put mixture in a pastry bag fitted with a #5 plain round tip. Pipe out in 1-inch balls on waxed paper. Place in freezer for 15 to 20 minutes until firm.

5 Sprinkle with powdered sugar and round the balls between the palms of your hands.

6 *To coat:* Chop chocolate for coating and melt in a double boiler over hot, not boiling, water. Temper the chocolate, according to instructions for tempering in Milk Chocolate Almond, steps 7 to 9 (page 143).

7 Using a fork, dip balls into the melted chocolate; set on a glazing tray or a tray lined with parchment. Set aside to cool. Serve at room temperature. (Color photo on page T.)

Chocolate Truffles Amaretto

Yields 20 truffles

8 oz.	milk chocolate
4 oz.	Crème Fraîche (recipe follows)
1 oz.	butter
1½ oz.	amaretto liqueur
12 oz.	white chocolate
1 oz.	milk chocolate, melted, for decorating

1 Chop chocolate and melt in the top of a double boiler over hot, not boiling, water.

2 Add the crème fraîche and butter; whisk together until smooth and butter and chocolate are melted.

3 Stir in the amaretto.

4 Cool mixture in refrigerator for 1 to 2 hours.

5 Using a pastry bag fitted with a #5 plain tip, pipe 1-inch balls on waxed paper.

6 Place in the freezer for 15 to 20 minutes until firm.

7 To coat: Chop 12 oz. of white chocolate and place in a stainless steel bowl over hot, not boiling water; stir continuously until chocolate melts.

8 Temper the chocolate, according to instructions for tempering in Milk Chocolate Almond, steps 7 to 9 (page 143).

9 Using a fork, dip balls in tempered white chocolate and place on parchment.

10 Decorate with 1 oz. of melted milk chocolate piped through a paper cone or a pastry bag fitted with a #00 tip. Refrigerate until needed.

Crème Fraîche

8 oz. heavy cream
¼ oz. buttermilk

1 Pour the cream into a glass jar and stir in the buttermilk; mix thoroughly or shake.

2 Cover tightly with plastic; let the mixture stand at room temperature for at least 8 hours or until it becomes thick.

3 Spoon the thickened cream into another jar; cover and refrigerate.

Use within 3 weeks.

Salad of Mallard Breast
with Asparagus and Truffle Vinaigrette

Serves 8

2	Bibb lettuces
4 oz.	lamb's tongue lettuce
1	radicchio
1	small curly chicory
2	mallards (3–3½ lbs. each)
½ lb.	tiny green asparagus
	salt to taste
8 oz.	Truffle Vinaigrette (page 39)
4 oz.	fresh morels or chanterelles
2	ripe tomatoes, blanched and peeled
	white pepper, freshly ground
¼ oz.	shallot, finely chopped
2 oz.	vegetable oil

1 Clean, wash, and dry the lettuce, radicchio, and chicory. Tear into small pieces. Cover and refrigerate until ready to use.

2 Debone the mallards; set aside the breasts. Cut up the leg meat and skin in ¼-inch dice.

3 If you use tiny asparagus, there is no need to peel them; cut in 4-inch pieces. Poach lightly in salted water; drain and place in a bowl. Marinate in some of the truffle vinaigrette.

4 Clean and halve the morels or chanterelles.

5 Halve the peeled tomatoes and remove the seeds; then cut the tomatoes into V-shaped wedges.

6 Cut the skin of the mallards and lightly season with salt and pepper. In a hot skillet, sear the breast, skin side down, until brown; then turn over, skin side up. Roast in a preheated 450°F oven for about 3 minutes until still rare. Set aside before slicing.

7 In the same skillet, sauté the diced leg and skin, seasoned with salt and pepper, until crisp. Remove from skillet and set aside.

8 Heat the oil in the skillet until very hot. Sauté the morels or chanterelles and shallot. Season with salt and pepper.

9 Mix the salad greens with the remaining vinaigrette.

10 *To serve*: Arrange greens nicely on the plates. Garnish with the tomatoes, asparagus, and crispy leg and skin. Slice the breast and place on the greens. Garnish with morels or chanterelles and mango slices. Serve warm. (Color photo on page C.)

Alexander Valley Vineyards Chardonnay—Sonoma, California

Salad of Mallard Breast is a difficult match for a wine because of the asparagus and the truffle vinaigrette. Since our dishes are tailored to wines, the chef maintains a mild taste to the vinaigrette dressing. People often associate duck with red wine. Chardonnay is the most full-bodied white wine and easily stands up to the complex flavors of the duck breast.

Lobster Ravioli

Serves 6

for FILLING

3	lobsters (1¼ lbs. each), cooked and removed from shell
12 oz.	fresh chanterelles
2 oz.	unsalted butter
1	shallot, chopped
3 oz.	Crème Fraîche (page 36)
	salt to taste
	white pepper, freshly ground
1	bunch chive, thinly cut

for RAVIOLI

48	thin won ton wrappers
1	egg yolk, lightly beaten

for LOBSTER SAUCE AND GARNISH

16 oz.	Lobster Stock (recipe follows)
4 oz.	unsalted butter, chilled
1	truffle, cut into julienne slices

1 *To make the filling*: Dice the lobster meat in ½-inch cubes.

2 Clean the chanterelles; sauté in butter in a saucepan. Add the shallot. Chop the mixture finely and return to the saucepan. Mix in the crème fraîche and quickly bring to a boil. Season with salt and pepper. Add the chive and lobster meat.

3 *To stuff the ravioli*: Lay won ton wrappers on a flat surface and brush half of them with the yolk. Place ¾ teaspoon of the filling in the middle and cover with the second wrapper. Press the edges to seal. Cut into rounds. (A quick way to do this: use the dull side of a round cookie cutter to mark the circle. Cut with a pastry cutter. You can cut the trimmings into strips or squares and freeze to drop into noodle soups.)

4 *To cook the ravioli and sauce*: Use half of the stock. Bring to a boil in a large pot and cook ravioli in boiling stock for 30 seconds; drain.

5 Reduce remaining half of the stock by half to 4 oz. Carefully whisk in the 4 oz. of butter so that the sauce binds well.

6 *To serve*: Place 3 ravioli on each plate. Cover with sauce and garnish with sliced truffle. (Color photo on page C.)

Chianti Classico, Ruffino Riserva Ducale—Tuscany, Italy
This medium-bodied red wine brings out the taste of the Lobster Ravioli. The acidity combines well with the lobster, and the San-giovese grape (the primary variety for this wine) has enough fruit to complement the ravioli. Dr. Am-brosio, the owner of Ruffino, rec-ommends the 1975, 1977, and 1979 vintages.

The taste of truffles cannot be compared with any other mush-room. The truffle grows under-ground and is very rare. A few slices give seasoning power to any dish. You can use truffles in sauces, goose liver terrines, pâtés, and salads. A truffle can be de-scribed as black and potato-shaped with a lot of humps.

LOBSTER STOCK

Use for lobster sauce, lobster bisque and lobster consommé.

Yields 1 quart

3 oz.	olive oil
2 lbs.	lobster bones, weak or oversized lobster
2 ea.	garlic cloves, crushed
2 oz.	shallot, chopped
4 oz.	leek, washed and sliced
8 oz.	vine-ripened tomato chopped
1 oz.	tomato paste
2 oz.	cognac
6 oz.	dry white wine
1½ qts.	water
2	bay leaves
1	fresh thyme sprig
10	white peppercorns
½ oz.	salt
1 qt.	White Fish Stock (page 154)

1 In a large iron skillet, gently heat the olive oil. Add the lobster bones, weak or oversized lobster, or shrimp shells, if using them. Sauté gently for 2 to 3 minutes, stirring constantly with a wooden spoon, without browning.

2 Stir in the garlic, shallot, and leek; continue to sauté for 2 minutes.

3 Add the tomato, tomato paste, and cognac. Flame the cognac.

4 When the flame subsides, pour in the wine and simmer gently until the wine evaporates and the liquid is reduced.

5 Add the water and very slowly bring to the boiling point, skimming off the foam and fat as they rise to the surface. Add the herbs, peppercorns, and salt. Simmer gently for 30 minutes.

6 Strain through a dampened cheesecloth directly into a saucepan. Bring to a boil and add the White Fish Stock. Simmer until reduced to 1 quart; cool.

7 Store in the refrigerator to use within 3 days; or divide into 2-cup quantities and freeze for up to 3 months.

Never wash lobster or any shellfish before cooking. When making the stock you can use weak lobster, oversized lobster, or the shells peeled off shrimps.

Truffle Vinaigrette

Serves 8

1 oz.	virgin olive oil
1 oz.	vegetable oil
1 oz.	sherry vinegar
1 oz.	truffle liquid (from the can)
1/16 oz.	truffle peelings (from the can), chopped (optional)
	salt
	white pepper, freshly ground

1 Combine the oils and vinegar in a bowl; whisk with a whip.

2 Add the truffle liquid and chopped peelings, if using.

3 Season with salt and pepper.

PRODUCE OF FRANCE

Chante-Alouette

APPELLATION HERMITAGE CONTRÔLÉE

MIS EN BOUTEILLE PAR

M. CHAPOUTIER S.A.

NÉGOCIANTS-ÉLEVEURS A TAIN L'HERMITAGE / DROME / FRANCE

CONTENTS 750 ml   ALCOHOL 14°/o BY VOL.

IMPORTED BY

Charles Lefranc Cellars

SAN JOSE, CALIFORNIA . SOLE AGENTS FOR U.S.A.

Hermitage, M. Chapoutier— Rhône Valley, France

This is a classic combination. A full-bodied Rhône wine and the taste of venison, although both are very distinct, make excellent complements for American Venison Two Ways. Hermitage is one of the longest-lasting wines in the world. The best recent vintages are 1976, 1978, and 1983. In this particular menu, the Hermitage is also served with the cheese course because there are very few wines that can follow it.

American Venison
—Two Ways—

with Sweet Potato Purée, Cheese Polenta, Sautéed Mushrooms, and Rye Crouton, Onion, and Bacon Garnish

Serves 8

for VENISON STEW MARINADE

1 lb.	leg of venison (fallow deer or axis)
8 oz.	dry red wine
4 oz.	port
2 oz.	shallot
1	fresh thyme sprig
1	fresh rosemary sprig
10	white peppercorns
5	juniper berries
½	orange rind
1	bay leaf
1/16 oz.	coriander seed
½	garlic clove
½ oz.	red wine vinegar

for STEW

2 oz.	vegetable oil
1 qt.	Brown Game Stock (made from venison bones and trimmings, recipe follows)
	salt
	white pepper, freshly ground
2 oz.	bitter chocolate

for ROAST VENISON LOIN

	Cheese Polenta (recipe follows)
	Sweet Potato Purée (recipe follows)
	Sautéed Mushrooms (recipe follows)
	Rye Crouton, Onion, and Bacon Garnish (recipe follows)
	pink peppercorns for garnish
3 lbs.	venison loin (fallow deer or axis)
3 oz.	vegetable oil
	salt
	white pepper, freshly ground

1 *To make the marinade and stew*: Bone and completely trim fat and skin off the leg of venison. Cut into 1½-inch cubes (Save the bone and trimmings to make Brown Game Stock). Combine all ingredients, except the venison cubes, to make a marinade. Place venison in the marinade; cover and let stand overnight.

2 Remove venison from the marinade and dry. Strain the marinade; save the vegetables and the marinade.

3 Season the venison with salt and pepper. In a casserole, heat the oil and sauté the venison until the juices start to flow. Take meat out of the casserole and set aside. Add the reserved vegetables to the casserole, sautéing until lightly browned.

4 Return the venison to the casserole and deglaze with part of the marinade, reducing the liquid until light caramel in color. Deglaze again; repeat this step several times, until the sauce has a nice rich color.

5 Pour in the brown game stock and cook till tender; remove the meat.

6 *To make the sauce*: Strain the sauce; reduce until you have the desired amount of liquid. Add the bitter chocolate. Strain and again place the venison in the sauce. Correct seasoning. Keep warm until needed.

7 *To prepare the roast loin*: Trim the venison loin. Season with salt and pepper.

8 Heat oil in roasting pan; quickly sear the loin on both sides to seal the juices. Place in a preheated 400°F oven for 6 to 7 minutes, keeping the venison rare. Remove from oven and let cool for 6 to 8 minutes.

9 *To serve*: Place the stew in the middle of a plate. Place the cheese polenta on one side of plate, garnish on the other side along with the sweet potato purée and sautéed mushrooms. Slice the loin and place halfway on top of the polenta. Garnish the stew with the croutons, bacon, and onion. Sprinkle with pink peppercorns. (Color photo on page D.)

(continued)

Sautéed Mushrooms

8 oz.	wild or regular mushrooms
3 oz.	unsalted butter, clarified
1 oz.	shallot, finely chopped
	salt
	white pepper, freshly ground
⅙ oz.	flat-leaf parsley, chopped
⅙ oz.	chive, finely cut

1 If using wild mushrooms, do not wash; otherwise the flavor will be lost. Clean and wash regular mushrooms. If very large, cut mushrooms in half lengthwise.

2 Heat butter in a skillet, sauté the shallot; then add the mushrooms and cook on very high heat for about 1 to 2 minutes. Season with salt and pepper.

3 Sprinkle with the herbs.

To clarify butter, use a large pot or casserole. On low heat, melt the butter until the milk product and the fat separate. The butter will foam, but the pot should be large enough to hold it; if not, the pot is too small, which will result in the butter boiling over (making a very messy stove that could cause a fire). When the foam sets, take the pot off the burner and separate the fat from the milk product by ladling the fat from the top. Strain through a fine Chinese strainer and refrigerate. Clarified butter is easier to cook with because it can be heated to a higher temperature than unclarified butter and will turn brown less easily when used for frying.

SWEET POTATO PURÉE

Serves 8

3 oz.	unsalted butter
1½ oz.	sugar
1	rind from a lemon
1	rind from an orange
1	Granny Smith apple, peeled and diced
1	ripe banana, peeled and sliced
4 oz.	water
4	sweet potatoes, peeled and diced
¼	cinnamon stick
	salt to taste
	white pepper, freshly ground

1 Heat half of the butter and add the sugar, stirring constantly. Add the lemon and orange rinds and the diced apple. Sauté until nicely carmelized.

2 Add the banana and water, the sweet potatoes, cinnamon stick, and a little salt.

3 Simmer until the sweet potatoes are tender. Reduce the liquid. Remove the cinnamon stick and rinds.

4 Press potato mixture through a fine sieve, or purée in a processor. Add the remaining half of the butter and correct the seasoning with salt and pepper. With a soup spoon, form quenelle shapes.

CHEESE POLENTA

Serves 8

1 pt.	milk
4 oz.	unsalted butter
4 oz.	yellow cornmeal
1½ oz.	Parmesan, grated
	salt to taste
	white pepper, freshly ground

1 In a saucepan, bring the milk to a boil; add half of the butter and slowly add the cornmeal, stirring constantly with a whisk.

2 Boil for about 3 minutes; then stir in half of the Parmesan.

3 Butter a flat pan and spread the cooked polenta ½-inch high. Cover with plastic or parchment paper so that it will not form a skin; let cool.

4 When needed, cut into rounds, half-moons, or other shapes. Sprinkle with the remaining butter and cheese. Bake at 375°F for 5 minutes.

Rye Crouton, Onion, and Bacon Garnish

4 oz.	rye bread slices
2 oz.	butter
4 oz.	small pearl onion, peeled
3 oz.	bacon
	salt
	pink peppercorns

1 Cut off the rye bread crust (save the crust to make bread crumbs). Then cut bread into ¼-inch cubes. Sauté in half of the butter until brown and crisp. Set aside on a paper towel.

2 In salted water, cook the onion for about 1 minute. Refresh in cold water; dry and sauté in the remaining butter until golden.

3 Cut bacon in strips and sauté until crisp; drain off the fat and reserve the bacon. Use pink peppercorns on top of venison stew when serving.

BROWN GAME STOCK

Venison, roebuck, pheasant, and other game may be used to prepare this stock.

Yields 2 quarts

4 oz.	olive oil
2½ lbs.	game bones, skin, and trimmings, cut into small pieces
3 oz.	carrot, diced
3 oz.	celery, diced
1	leek, washed and sliced
3 oz.	onion, diced
1	garlic clove
3 oz.	tomato paste
8 oz.	dry red wine
4 qts.	cold water
4	bay leaves
1	fresh rosemary sprig
1	fresh thyme sprig
10	juniper berries, crushed
1 oz.	salt
16 oz.	Brown Veal Stock (page 153)

1 Heat a roasting pan or heavy skillet and add the oil, chopped bones, and trimmings. Cook and stir until slightly browned.

2 Roast in a preheated oven at 350°F for 1 hour or until bones are evenly browned.

3 Add the carrot and celery. Continue roasting for 3 minutes; then add the leek, onion, and garlic.

4 Skim off the excess fat and add the tomato paste. Roast for a few minutes.

5 Deglaze with half of the wine and reduce slowly. Repeat this step with the remaining wine.

6 Remove from the oven and add 1 quart of the water; bring to a boil. Skim off the excess fat.

7 Transfer bones and liquid to a larger stockpot. Add the remaining water, and the herbs and spices.

8 Bring to a boil and simmer gently for about 1½ hours, skimming off excess fat occasionally.

9 Strain through cheesecloth directly into a saucepan. Stir in the brown veal stock and reduce over low heat until the desired quantity is obtained.

All the recipes for stocks and sauces call for vegetables, such as onions, leeks, celery, and carrots. Always use the end cuts from these vegetables for stocks and sauces. Use the central portion of the vegetable for the main dish. The same rule applies when recipes call for mushroom heads; save the stems for stocks.

When cooking any kind of bones for a stock, never cook longer than the recipe suggests. Overcooking will disintegrate the bones and make the stock cloudy and also make it taste like gelatin. And to have a really clear stock, be sure it is free of all fat. Skim off all foam and fat as you slowly bring the stock to a boil. A little patience when making the stock makes clear stock to use in your sauces and soups.

Wehlener Sonnenuhr Auslese, J.J. Prüm—Mosel, Germany
The degree of sweetness usually associated with Auslese wines, especially the lighter-style Mosels, highlights the acidity present in the Tropical Fruit Soup. The 1983 and 1985 vintages are recommended.

This is the only menu in which I suggest two wines for the same course. Both are California wines with Sautéed Hudson Valley Duck Liver. Certain sweet wines will complement the texture of duck liver as will dry, full-bodied white wines. What's your preference?

Robert Mondavi Chardonnay—Napa Valley, California
The Robert Mondavi Chardonnay is a full-bodied, dry white wine. This wine was aged in oak barrels, which adds extra flavor and depth. The Mondavi wines have always been considered "blue chip," and the winery is constantly experimenting to improve the quality of all California wines.

Chateau St. Jean, Late Harvest Johannisberg Riesling—Sonoma, California
Late harvest means that the grapes were kept on the vine for a longer period of time to increase their sugar concentration. This particular wine contains 7.2 percent residual sugar, which makes it equivalent in sweetness to a German Beerenauslese. Château St. Jean is one of the top producers of late-harvest wines in California.

THE
cellar
IN THE SKY

Chef's Canapés
Sautéed Hudson Valley Duck Liver with Truffles
Château St. Jean Late Harvest Johannisberg Riesling
— or —
Robert Mondavi Chardonnay
Glazed Lobster Consommé
Fillet of Striped Bass with Whole-Grain Mustard Sauce
— Meursault, Louis Jadot —
Herb-Crusted Roast Loin of Lamb
Ratatouille of Small Vegetables
and Skillet-Fried Potatoes
— Château Pichon-La Lande —
International Cheeseboard
— Torres, Gran Coronas —
Mille Feuille with Wild Strawberries
— Bernkasteler Graben Auslese, Dr. Thanisch —
Petits Fours
Colombian Coffee

107th FLOOR/ONE WORLD TRADE CENTER/NEW YORK, N.Y. 10048/(212) 938-1111

Sautéed Hudson Valley Duck Liver with Truffles

Serves 8

2 lbs.	fresh Hudson Valley duck liver (foie gras de canard)
	salt
	white pepper, freshly ground
	red leaf lettuce
	lamb's tongue lettuce
	curly chicory
4	large artichokes (only the buttons), cooked
6 oz.	Truffle Vinaigrette (page 39)
1 oz.	fresh truffles
2 oz.	unsalted butter, clarified
8	quail eggs
1 oz.	vegetable oil
½ oz.	fresh chervil leaves

1   Clean, skin, and devein the duck liver. Cut into ½-inch-thick slices, one per person. (Save the end cuts for other dishes.) Season liver slices with salt and pepper.

2   Wash all the lettuce and chicory and tear into small pieces.

3   Thinly slice the artichoke buttons.

4   Toss the lettuce with the truffle vinaigrette.

5   Arrange a ring of artichoke slices nicely on 8 large plates.

6   Slice the truffles thinly and dress over the artichoke slices. Place the salad in the middle of the plate.

7   In a very hot iron skillet, sauté the liver in butter until it is still pink. Place liver on a dry towel.

8   In a small skillet, fry the quail eggs in the oil.

9   *To serve*: Place liver on top of the lettuce. Top with a fried quail egg on each plate. Garnish with fresh chervil leaves. Serve warm. (Color photo on page D.)

**Meursault, Louis Jadot—
Burgundy, France**
Meursault is the name of a village in the Burgundy region. This white wine is made from 100 percent Chardonnay, and I chose it to go with the Fillet of Striped Bass because of its excellent balance of acidity and fruit. The sauce is made with Dijon mustard, also from Burgundy. Louis Jadot is one of the top shippers and negociants of Burgundian wines. I recommend the 1983 and 1985 vintages.

**Château Pichon-Lalande—
Bordeaux, France**
This second-growth Bordeaux wine is, in my opinion, one of the top-ten châteaus. The main grape is Cabernet Sauvignon. This is a classic combination and also one of my favorites. I would love to have this Herb-crusted Roast Loin of Lamb with a mature Pichon-Lalande, such as a 1961 or 1966 vintage. Unfortunately, these particular wines are extremely hard to find and very expensive. The more recent vintages of 1978 or 1979 will still bring out the flavor of the lamb.

Herb-Crusted Roast Loin of Lamb
with Garlic Confit, Ratatouille of Small Vegetables, and Skillet-Fried Potatoes

Serves 8

1	lamb loin left whole
	salt
	white pepper, freshly ground
2 oz.	vegetable oil

for HERB CRUST

6 oz.	unsalted butter
½ oz.	fresh thyme, finely chopped
½ oz.	fresh rosemary, finely chopped
½ oz.	flat-leaf parsley, finely chopped

(continued)

Garlic Confit

    20 large garlic cloves,
       unpeeled
    1 qt. water
    1 qt. milk
    1 oz. unsalted butter
    2 oz. sugar

1 Refresh the garlic in cold water. In a saucepan, bring one-third the water and one-third the milk to a boil with the garlic; drain.

2 Repeat the blanching twice more, using all the water and milk.

3 Heat the butter in a skillet and stir in the blanched garlic cloves; then add the sugar, mixing well. Preheat oven to 375°F and bake for 15 minutes.

For some dishes of the new culinary trends, small (baby) vegetables, ferns, and sprouts are highly prized. Try some of the following in your dishes: yellow squash or zucchini—with their flowers still on; small eggplants—purple or white; small artichokes; tiny asparagus—raw or lightly sautéed; fiddlehead ferns—available fresh only for a few weeks in April or May; sprouts—azuki, or enoki, soy, or mung bean sprouts, lightly steamed, sautéed in butter, or raw. All of these fruits and vegetables can be eaten raw as crudités with dipping sauces or as garnishes for appetizers or entrées.

    ½ oz. chive, finely sliced
    ¼ oz. chervil
      ½ garlic clove, crushed or finely chopped
    2 oz. white bread crumbs
         salt, to taste
         white pepper, freshly ground
         Lamb Wine Sauce (recipe follows)
         Garlic Confit (recipe follows)
         Ratatouille of Small Vegetables (recipe
            follows)
         Skillet-Fried Potatoes (recipe follows)
         Fresh rosemary and thyme sprigs for
            garnish

1 *To prepare the lamb loin*: Completely debone and devein the lamb. Save the trimmings for the sauce (recipe follows). Season the loin with salt and pepper. Heat the oil in the skillet and sear the loin for one minute on each side. Remove and set aside to cool.

2 *To make the herb crust*: Whip the butter until very fluffy. Add all the herbs and garlic, mixing well. Stir in the bread crumbs. Season with salt and pepper.

3 Place the herb mixture on top of the *cool* loin and firmly squeeze to make a crust.

4 Bake in a preheated 375°F oven for about 8 minutes till slightly brown. Remove from oven. Let rest for 5 minutes before slicing.

5 *To slice*: Use a long, thin knife to avoid breaking the crust.

6 *To serve*: Ladle the sauce on 8 heated plates. Place 2 slices of meat on top. Arrange the garlic confit, ratatouille and potato garnishes nicely around the meat and sauce. Slip sprays of rosemary and thyme under the garlic. Serve hot. (Color photo on page E.)

RATATOUILLE OF SMALL VEGETABLES

    4 oz. small yellow squash, diced or sliced
            lengthwise
    4 oz. small zucchini, diced or sliced lengthwise
    4 oz. small eggplant, diced
      3 ripe tomatoes, peeled, seeded, and diced
    ½ oz. onion, diced
      ½ garlic clove
    2 oz. olive oil
      ½ fresh rosemary sprig, chopped
      ½ thyme sprig, chopped
         salt
         white pepper, freshly ground

1 Prepare the vegetables as indicated (page 46).

2 In a hot skillet, heat the olive oil and sauté the vegetables, herbs and seasonings. Serve hot.

SKILLET-FRIED POTATOES

1 lb.	medium potatoes, peeled
3 oz.	unsalted butter, clarified
	salt
	white pepper, freshly ground
8	cherry tomatoes

1 Peel, wash, and thinly slice the potatoes; wash again.

2 In a small skillet (2½-inches in diameter), heat the butter. Lay the potato slices, one at a time, into the hot butter to make a pinwheel effect, using 10 or 11 slices at a time. The slices will adhere as you fry the potatoes. Turn and fry on the other side. Drain on paper towels and continue frying the potato slices.

3 Place the fried potato pinwheels on a baking sheet. Preheat oven to 350°F and bake for about 8 minutes until golden.

4 Cut off the stem side of the tomatoes to make them flat. Set a tomato in the middle of each potato pinwheel. Bake for another 3 minutes or until the tomatoes are soft. Serve hot.

LAMB WINE SAUCE

all	lamb bones and trimmings (reserved from the loin), chopped into small pieces
3 oz.	vegetable oil
2 oz.	shallot, diced
1	garlic clove, crushed
6 oz.	dry red wine
3 oz.	port
16 oz.	Brown Lamb Stock (page 155)
1	fresh thyme sprig
1	fresh rosemary sprig

1 In a heavy skillet heat the oil; brown the bones and trimmings in hot oil till evenly browned. Add the shallots and garlic, and cook for about half a minute.

2 Deglaze with the red wine and the port. Stir in the lamb stock and herbs. Simmer for about 30 minutes; degrease occasionally. Strain through a Chinese strainer.

3 Reduce sauce to the amount needed.

de Ladoucette

Mis en bouteille par de LADOUCETTE
AU CHATEAU DU NOZET, POUILLY-S -LOIRE (NIEVRE)
ALCOHOL 12.5 % BY VOLUME   STILL WHITE WINE
CONTENTS 750 ml (25.4 FL. OZ.)   PRODUCE OF FRANCE

EXCLUSIVE IMPORTER
INTERNATIONAL VINTAGE WINE COMPANY
HARTFORD, CT 06101

**Pouilly-Fumé, Ladoucette—
Loire Valley, France**
Salmon is a fish with which I
would have no problem serving
a red wine, but not in this case.
In this menu, the salmon is
served with a beurre blanc sauce,
which originated in the Loire Valley. Pouilly-Fumé is made from
100 percent Sauvignon Blanc
grapes and is considered the
fullest-bodied white wine of
the Loire Valley. Ladoucette is one
of the best producers. Look for
the 1983 and 1985 vintages.

**Veuve Clicquot, Brut non-vin-
tage—Champagne, France**
Sparkling wine is, for many people, the all-purpose, apéritif wine.
(See the discussion of Champagne on page 67.) Veuve Clicquot brut is a full-bodied, dry
Champagne.

Scallop of Salmon with Soy Beurre Blanc and Azuki Sprouts

Serves 8

5 lbs.	whole salmon
	salt to taste
	white pepper, freshly ground
6 oz.	unsalted butter
2 oz.	dry white wine
4 oz.	White Fish Stock (page 154)
4 oz.	carrot, cut in fine strips
8 oz.	fennel, cut in fine strips
½ lb.	azuki bean sprouts or substitute other bean sprouts
14 oz.	Beurre Blanc (page 154)
¾ oz.	soy sauce
1 oz.	chive, cut in long, fine slivers

1 Clean, skin, and bone the salmon; cut into eight 7-oz. scallops. Season salmon with salt and pepper.

2 Spread half of the butter in a casserole; set the salmon in the casserole. Add the wine and fish stock. Stir the carrot and fennel strips into the casserole and heat gently. Poach for about 4 to 5 minutes.

3 In a skillet, sauté the sprouts in the remaining butter for about 1 minute; season lightly with salt and pepper.

4 *To make the sauce*: Combine the beurre blanc and soy sauce (avoid adding salt; soy sauce already has a very high salt content).

5 *To serve*: Ladle the soy beurre blanc on the plates. Set the poached scallop of salmon on the sauce. Garnish with the fennel and carrot strips with the sprouts around the salmon. Sprinkle with the chive slivers. (Color photo on page F.)

Roast Breast
of Squab
with
Foie Gras Sauce
Stuffed Savoy Cabbage
and
Small Vegetables and
Potato Mushrooms

Serves 8

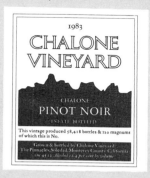

4 oz	whole squabs
	Stuffed Savoy Cabbage (recipe follows)
	Small Vegetables and Potato Mushrooms (recipe follows)
	Foie Gras Sauce (recipe follows)
	salt to taste
	white pepper, freshly grated
1 oz.	vegetable oil

1   Separate the squab breasts from the legs. Use the legs to make the stuffed cabbage (recipe follows). Prepare the potatoes and sauce before cooking the squab.

2   Season the squab breasts with salt and pepper. On a burner, heat the oil in a roasting pan until very hot. Sauté the squab breasts until quite brown on both sides.

3   Preheat oven to 375°F and roast for 3 to 5 minutes. The breasts should be rare. Rest for 5 minutes before cutting the meat from the bone.

4   Slice the meat with a very sharp knife, holding one hand on top of the meat and slicing nearly horizontally (as slicing smoked salmon).

5   To serve, ladle some sauce on each heated plate. Set the sliced breast on the sauce. Nicely garnish with all the vegetables around the squab.

Foie Gras

1 oz.	shallot, chopped
½ oz.	unsalted butter
4 oz.	dry red wine
2 oz.	Madeira
1 pt.	Brown Game Stock (page 43)
2 oz.	foie gras (duck liver, end pieces)
	salt to taste
	white pepper, freshly ground

1   Sauté the shallot in the butter. Add the wines and boil until reduced.
2   Add the stock and reduce to 2 cups.
3   Pour the sauce into a blender; add the foie gras, piece by piece, while mixing.
4   Strain and reheat carefully, simmering, not boiling, the sauce. Correct the seasoning with salt and pepper.

(continued)

Brunello di Montalcino, Fattoria dei Barbi—Tuscany, Italy
This is the king of Tuscan wines. Although made with the same grape as a Chianti, it has much more flavor, depth, and longevity. This wine can hold up to medium- and strong-tasting cheeses but might overpower a lighter-style cheese. Fattoria dei Barbi is the name of the producer. Look for the 1978, 1979, and 1981 vintages.

Château Suduiraut—Sauternes, France
I do not believe there is any sweet wine that will go with ice cream, except possibly certain Sherries and Ports. Think of this menu as having two desserts: the Château Suduiraut and the Gâteau Pithiviers with Almond Ice Cream. Depending upon the year, this wine can be medium-to-full bodied with a sweet, balanced richness. Château Suduiraut is one of my favorite Sauternes. I recommend the 1975, 1976, 1979, and 1981 vintages.

STUFFED SAVOY CABBAGE

4	squab legs, deboned
2 oz.	unsalted butter
½ oz.	shallot, diced
3 oz.	mushrooms (chanterelles, if in season), quartered
1	small savoy cabbage
6 oz.	foie gras (duck liver, end pieces), diced
	salt to taste
	white pepper, freshly ground

1 Bone the squab legs and trim the meat. In a skillet, sauté in the butter. Remove the squab legs and place in a bowl.

2 In the same skillet, sauté the shallot and mushroom. Add to the bowl with the sautéed squab legs.

3 Sauté the diced foie gras in the same skillet. Add to the bowl and mix. Season filling with salt and pepper and set aside until needed.

4 *Prepare the cabbage*: In salted water, blanch the cabbage leaves so that they are soft. Drain and dry them with a towel.

5 *To stuff*: place a spoonful of the filling on each cabbage leaf; wrap the leaf, making a small roll. Continue until all the leaves are stuffed.

6 Set cabbage rolls in a buttered baking pan and bake for 5 minutes at about 325°F. Keep warm until needed.

SMALL VEGETABLES AND POTATO MUSHROOMS

8	white-skinned new potatoes
12 oz.	small carrot
6 oz.	scallion
8	small artichokes
1 oz.	lemon juice
3 oz.	unsalted butter
¼ oz.	pink peppercorns
1	flat-leaf parsley sprig

1 Cut each potato to resemble a mushroom with a cap and stem. You can do this with a small knife; or you can use our method: Push a round cookie cutter into the potato; cut around the handle to make the stem part and shape the cap; cut off the stem end to make it straight.

2 Leaving some of the stem on, peel the carrot; cook in a salted water in a saucepan; drain

3 Trim the scallion and blanch in salted water; drain.

4 Clean the artichokes; cook in salted water and lemon juice; drain.

5 Shortly before serving, sauté the potatoes in the butter; then add the carrot and scallion. Sprinkle with pink peppercorns and garnish with the parsley leaves.

Baked
Red Snapper
with
Confit of Vegetables
Fried Onion Rings,
Pepper Tartlets,
and
Two Pepper Sauces

Serves 8

	Confit of Vegetables (recipe follows)
	Fried Onion Rings (recipe follows)
	Pepper Tartlets (recipe follows)
	Two Pepper Sauces (recipe follows)
4 (1½ lbs. each)	red snapper
	salt to taste
	white pepper, freshly ground
3 oz.	olive oil
12 oz.	White Fish Stock (page 154)

1   Before preparing the snapper, make the vegetable and onion garnishes, tartlets, and sauce.

2   Scale and fillet the snapper but leave skin on; cut snapper diagonally in half.

3   Season and rub with olive oil.

4   Place snapper in a flat pan with skins up and add the stock.

5   Bake in preheated 375°F oven for about 7 minutes or until tender.

6   *To serve:* Place 2 snapper fillets, skin side up, on each heated plate. Arrange the vegetables in alternating and overlapping circles—eggplant, tomato, zucchini, tomato, eggplant—on each side of the fillets. Spoon some green pepper sauce and red pepper sauce on each plate and top each with the contrasting-colored tartlet. Garnish with onion rings. (Color photo on page G.)

Chassagne-Montrachet, Louis Latour—Burgundy, France
Chasagne-Montrachet is the name of a village in the Burgundy region. I have always found that white wines of Burgundy—especially the village wines—go well with a fish appetizer course. The two pepper sauces served with the red snapper are mild in taste, not overpowering enough to interfere with the wine. Look for the 1983 and 1985 vintages.

(continued)

Fresh herbs enrich your cooking with their magical flavors. When unavailable, you can substitute dried herbs in smaller amounts. For a sprig of parsley or thyme, for example, grasp as much dried herb as you can hold between your thumb and forefinger. But don't just drop it into the food. Rub it in your palms to release all the aromas.

To make Two Pepper Sauces, follow the recipe for Red Pepper Sauce (page 30). Substitute White Fish Stock (page 154) for the White Veal Stock. Repeat the exact recipe, but use a green bell pepper the second time. You should then have a green and a red sauce.

CONFIT OF VEGETABLES

1	*medium zucchini*
1	*small eggplant*
4	*medium tomatoes*
3 oz.	*olive oil*
1	*fresh thyme sprig, chopped*
	salt to taste
	white pepper, freshly ground

1 Cut zucchini, eggplant, and tomatoes into thin slices.

2 Alternately layer the vegetables in a casserole, seasoning and sprinkling with olive oil, salt, thyme, and pepper between layers.

3 Bake in preheated oven at 375°F for 4 minutes.

FRIED ONION RINGS

2	*medium onions*
2 oz.	*all-purpose flour*
5 oz.	*vegetable oil*

1 Peel the onions and slice into very thin rings.

2 Mix with the flour.

3 In a skillet, heat the oil and fry the rings till crisp. Set on paper towels to dry. Serve hot.

PEPPER TARTLETS

1	*red bell pepper*
1	*green bell pepper*
2 oz.	*unsalted butter*
4 oz.	*heavy cream*
	salt to taste
	white pepper, freshly ground
	Quiche Dough (recipe follows)

1 Finely dice the red and green peppers, but keep the pepper colors separated.

2 In separate skillets, sauté the peppers in heated butter until soft. Add half of the heavy cream to each skillet; stir and reduce. Season to taste.

3 Prepare the Quiche Dough. Roll and cut dough to fit 1½-inch tartlet shells. Bake the pastry shells for 8 minutes or until done.

4 Fill the shells with the peppers before serving, keeping colors separated to make red and green tartlets. Serve hot.

QUICHE DOUGH

Yields dough for 16 tartlets

8 oz.	unsalted butter, chilled	pinch	salt
12 oz.	all-purpose flour	4 oz.	cold water or milk

1 Cut the chilled butter into cubes.

2 In a bowl, rub butter into flour with fingertips, leaving pieces of butter not fully blended. Add the salt.

3 Add cold water or milk, mixing thoroughly, but do not overwork.

4 Wrap the dough in plastic and refrigerate for half an hour before using.

5 Roll out on floured board and cut into desired shapes. Bake as directed in the recipe you are preparing.

Veal Loin Steak with Grapes, Chanterelles, and Fresh Corncakes

Serves 10

10 (5 oz. each)	veal loin steaks
½ oz.	salt
	white pepper, freshly ground
5 oz.	white grapes, peeled
5 oz.	red grapes, peeled
6 oz.	unsalted butter
2 oz.	sugar
20 oz.	chanterelles, fresh
8 oz.	walnut oil
½ oz.	shallot, chopped
	Fresh Corncakes (recipe follows)

1 Season the steaks with salt and pepper. In a skillet, sauté the steaks in 3 oz. of the butter, but let the interior of the meat remain pink.

2 Sauté the grapes in 2 oz. of the butter. Stir in the sugar and cook until the sugar dissolves.

3 Sauté the chanterelles in the walnut oil and remaining butter; then add the shallot and season with salt and pepper.

4 *To serve:* Ladle sauce onto the heated plates. Place the steaks on the sauce. Garnish with grapes, chanterelles, and corncakes.

BOUCHARD PÈRE & FILS
GEVREY-CHAMBERTIN
APPELLATION GEVREY-CHAMBERTIN CONTROLÉE

MIS EN BOUTEILLE PAR LA MAISON
BOUCHARD PÈRE & FILS, NÉGOCIANT AU CHATEAU BEAUNE (COTE-D'OR)
PRODUCE OF FRANCE   RED BURGUNDY WINE
ALCOHOL 13% BY VOLUME   CONT. 750 ML
PRODUCED AND BOTTLED BY: BOUCHARD PÈRE & FILS, BEAUNE
IMPORTED BY: INTERNATIONAL VINTAGE WINE CO. HARTFORD CT.

Gevrey-Chambertin, Bouchard Père & Fils—Burgundy, France
Gevrey-Chambertin is another village in the Burgundy region, known only for its red wines. It is considered one of the best village wines in all of Burgundy. This wine is made from 100 percent Pinot Noir grapes and is medium in style, which matches the texture of the veal loin. Bouchard Père & Fils is the producer of this wine. I recommend the 1979 and 1983 vintages.

(continued)

Tarragon: A perennial plant. The fresh or dried leaves are used to flavor a variety of dishes.

Amarone, Bertani—Veneto, Italy

Amarone is one of my favorite wines, but it is extremely difficult to match with food. Its high alcohol (sometimes as high as 16 percent) tends to overpower even hearty meat dishes. When Amarone is served at the Cellar in the Sky, it is always with the cheeseboard. In my opinion, Bertani is the best producer of this particular wine, which can easily age for 25 years. Among recent vintages, the best are 1974, 1977, and 1979.

Before you begin this recipe, have the following prepared in advance: Almond Paste, Raspberry Sauce, Pear Sorbet, and Hippen Shells. Then the assembly is quick.

FRESH CORNCAKES

12 oz.	fresh corn kernels
4 oz.	unsalted butter
½ oz.	red bell pepper, diced
½ oz.	green bell pepper, diced
8 oz.	half-and-half (cream and milk)
5	eggs
3 oz.	all-purpose flour
2 oz.	fresh tarragon, chopped
6 oz.	unsalted butter

1   Simmer corn kernels in the 4 oz. of butter. Add the green and red peppers, and sauté; let cool.

2   In a bowl, combine the half-and-half and eggs. Whisk in the flour, a little at a time, to make a thick batter that can be dropped from a spoon.

3   Add the sautéed corn and the tarragon.

4   In a skillet, melt the 6 oz. of butter. Drop corn batter from a spoon into the hot butter, as you would make small pancakes. Fry corncakes on each side until golden.

5   Set corncakes aside and keep warm.

Pear Crepe with Almonds and Pear Sorbet

Serves 10

10	ripe pears
20 oz.	unsalted butter, clarified
6 oz.	almonds, chopped
6 oz.	almond paste (available in specialty shops)
10	egg roll wrappers
2	eggs, lightly beaten
3 oz.	fresh raspberries
3 oz.	fresh strawberries
3 oz.	fresh blueberries
6 oz.	sugar
8 oz.	Raspberry Sauce (recipe follows)
18 oz.	Pear Sorbet (recipe follows)
10	Hippen Shells (small) (page 35)
20	fresh mint leaves for garnish

1 *To make the filling*: Peel and core the pears. Cut pears in ½-inch cubes. In a saucepan, sauté pears lightly in half of the butter for 2 to 3 minutes; set aside to cool.

2 Combine the sautéed pears, almonds, and almond paste.

3 *To stuff the wrappers*: Hold each wrapper with a point facing you. Place a spoonful of filling towards the front point. Cover with the point nearest you; cover with each side point and roll back, sealing all edges with the beaten eggs.

4 *To fry*: Heat the butter in a skillet. Fry each roll, turning to fry on all sides. Drain on paper towels.

5 In a bowl, sprinkle the berries with sugar; marinate for a few minutes.

6 *To serve*: Dress berries on top of the raspberry sauce. Scoop pear sorbet into the hippen shells. Garnish with mint leaves.

PEAR SORBET

Serves 8

4 oz.	water
4 oz.	sugar
¼	cinnamon stick
5	whole cloves
3	pears, peeled and diced
½ oz.	William Birne's pear liqueur or brandy

1 In a saucepan, bring water, sugar, cinnamon, and cloves to a boil; stir till sugar dissolves. Boil for about 3 minutes.

2 Strain the sauce over diced pears in another saucepan; simmer pears for about 2 minutes.

3 Remove cinnamon and cloves; mix pears and syrup in a blender until smooth. Stir in the pear liqueur.

4 Freeze in a sorbet machine or a freezer tray.

SPECIAL SELECT LATE HARVEST
Joseph Phelps Vineyards

Napa Valley
Johannisberg Riesling

Raspberry Sauce

Serves 8

7 oz.	fresh or frozen raspberries
4 oz.	Simple Syrup (page 63)
½	lemon, squeezed for the juice

1 Combine the fresh raspberries and syrup in a blender and mix until very smooth. If you use frozen raspberries, add less syrup, since they already are sweetened. Strain the sauce through a Chinese strainer.

2 Gradually add the lemon juice, adjusting the amount, depending on the fruit acidity. Taste and add more syrup, if needed.

3 A touch of Grand Marnier or raspberry liqueur can be added for flavor. Raspberry Sauce can be served with tarts, cakes, and cheesecake.

Joseph Phelps Late Harvest Riesling—Napa Valley, California

Joseph Phelps Winery is one of the top wine producers in Napa, making both excellent red and white wines. For the Pear Crepe with Almonds and Sorbet, I suggest the 1980 vintage, which has 16.3 percent residual sugar. It puts this sweet white Riesling on a par with a German Trockenbeerenauslese.

THE cellar IN THE SKY

∞ Chef's Canapés ∞
Seasonal Salad with Magret of Duck
Mussel Bisque with Cilantro
Freshly Smoked Salmon with Champagne,
Beurre Blanc and Caviar
— Moet and Chandon, Brut Non Vintage —
Côte de Boeuf
with Bordelaise Sauce and Vegetable Charlotte
— Jordan Cabernet Sauvignon —
International Cheeseboard
— Château Leoville-Las Cases —
Hot Glazed Fig Tart
— Niersteiner Oelberg Beerenauslese, R. Senfter —
Petits Fours
∞ Colombian Coffee ∞

107th FLOOR/ONE WORLD TRADE CENTER/NEW YORK, N.Y. 10048/(212) 938-1111

Cilantro or fresh coriander is a fragrant leafy herb useful in cooking and as a garnish.

Mussel Bisque with Cilantro

Serves 8

3 lbs.	mussels, washed and cleaned
2 oz.	shallot, peeled and chopped
6 oz.	unsalted butter
16 oz.	dry white wine
40 oz.	White Fish Stock (page 154)
dashes	Worcestershire sauce
2	bay leaves
10	white peppercorns
16 oz.	heavy cream
	salt to taste
	white pepper, freshly ground
1	cilantro (fresh coriander) sprig

1 Wash the mussels twice in cold water so that no sand is left. Pull the beards off the shells.

2 In a saucepan, sauté the shallots in the butter; add the mussels, wine, and fish stock. Stir in the bay leaves, peppercorns, and salt; cook for about 20 minutes. Strain the soup into another saucepan.

3 Set the mussels aside; when cool, separate the mussel meat from the shells. Use some mussels as a garnish in the bisque; or, if you prefer the bisque plain, save the mussels for a salad.

4 Bring the soup to a boil and add the heavy cream. Correct the seasonings with salt and pepper and add a few dashes of Worcestershire sauce. If the soup is too thin, dilute a half teaspoon of cornstarch in a little cold water and stir it into the boiling bisque.

5 When serving, sprinkle with small cilantro leaves.

Côte de Boeuf and Vegetable Charlotte with Bordelaise Sauce

Serves 8

4   *côte de boeuf, cut from prime ribs of beef, fat trimmed*
6 oz.   *vegetable oil*
       salt
1 oz.   *cracked black peppercorns*
16 oz.   *bone marrow, in the bone, cut in 1-inch pieces*
1 oz.   *fresh sage*
12 oz.   *Bordelaise Sauce (page 156)*
       Vegetable Charlotte (recipe follows)

1   Cut and trim the ribs; each rib should be about 26 oz. and 1½ to 1¾ inches thick, with the bone and fat trimmed. Season the ribs with salt and half of the cracked peppercorns.

2   In a heavy roasting pan, heat the oil.

3   Place the ribs in the hot oil and sear on each side for about 2 minutes.

4   Roast in a preheated 400°F oven for about 15 minutes or longer, depending on the degree that you want your meat cooked.

5   Remove from the pan; let rest for 10 minutes before carving.

6   Slice the bone marrow; or you can ask the butcher to cut into 1-inch pieces. Sear the marrow on a grill and roast in a hot oven for 2 minutes or till the bones are very hot. Tuck sage leaves into the marrow for garnish.

7   Cut the beef from the bone and trim off the excess fat. Lightly slice diagonally across the meat grain. Reserve 3 generous beef slices per guest.

8   To assemble the dish, ladle the sauce on each heated plate, and place the beef on top. Arrange the vegetable charlotte and garnished bone marrow around the beef and sauce. Sprinkle the vegetable charlotte with white pepper and the beef with cracked black peppercorns. (Color photo on page F.)

Jordan Cabernet Sauvignon—Sonoma, California
I can think of at least 500 different wines to serve with this Côte de Boeuf with Bordelaise Sauce. I chose the Jordan Cabernet Sauvignon because of its consistent quality, especially its balance of fruit and tannin even in a recent vintage. With Côte de Boeuf, I would serve either a Cabernet Sauvignon from California or an aged red Bordeaux wine from France.

(continued)

VEGETABLE CHARLOTTE

½	savoy cabbage head
16 oz.	carrot
14 oz.	celeriac
8 oz.	heavy cream
1	egg
1	egg yolk
	salt
	white pepper, freshly ground
3 oz.	unsalted butter
	pink peppercorns

1   Wash and separate the cabbage leaves; blanch the leaves in boiling water and drain; set aside.

2   Peel the carrot and celeriac; cut both into 1¼-inch-long and ⅛-inch-thick sticks, saving all the end cuts.

3   In a saucepan, cook the end cuts with a little water and the heavy cream until tender and most of the liquid has evaporated. Purée in a food processor. Add the egg and egg yolk. Season with salt and pepper to taste.

4   Butter 8 small forms (about 1¾ inches high and 1½ inches in diameter; lay a blanched cabbage leaf on the bottom of each form. Alternating the vegetables by color, place the carrot and celeriac sticks around the inside wall of the forms (the vegetables should stick because of the butter). Fill the forms with the vegetable purée. Cover the forms with aluminum foil.

5   Pour a half-inch of water on the bottom of a roasting pan. Set the forms in the pan.

6   Preheat oven to 350°F. Bake about 25 minutes. Remove from the oven and let rest for 5 minutes. When ready to serve, unmould the forms directly on the serving plates. Garnish with pink peppercorns. Serve warm.

Sancerre, Château de Sancerre—Loire Valley, France

This pot-au-feu is made with salmon. The sauce is made with fish stock, cream, and it is garnished with pink pepper, which adds a light sweetness. Sancerre is a medium-bodied wine made from 100 percent Sauvignon Blanc grapes. It has a higher than usual acidity because of its northern location in the Loire Valley. This acidity brings out the taste of the salmon and holds up to the cream sauce. I recommend the 1983 and 1985 vintages.

Châteauneuf-du-Pape, Paul Jaboulet Aîné—Rhône Valley, France

This is a wine I find difficult to match with the Cellar in the Sky menu. Because of its southern location, Châteauneuf-du-Pape is a full-bodied, dry red wine with an alcohol content around 13 percent. It needs many years of aging before it is ready to drink and recent vintages are high in tannin as well as alcohol, which overpower most foods with the exceptions of venison or cheese. Paul Jaboulet Aîné is one of the best producers of Rhône Valley wine. Look for the 1976 and 1978 vintages to drink now; for aging, choose the 1983 vintage.

Beaulieu, Cabernet Sauvignon—Napa Valley, California

Beaulieu makes three different styles of Cabernet Sauvignon wine. The first level is called Beau Tour. The next level of quality is Beaulieu Rutherford. The third and highest level is the Beaulieu Georges de La Tour Private Reserve. With the Roast Loin of Veal, I chose the Beaulieu Rutherford, which is made from 100 percent Cabernet Sauvignon grapes. In my opinion, this is one of the best values in Cabernets from California.

Schloss Vollrads Auslese—Rheingau, Germany

Rheingau is considered the best area for the production of high-quality German wines. This Schloss Vollrads, which is made with the Riesling grape variety, is full in body but not cloyingly sweet. It blends nicely with the acidity in the Feuillette of Mixed Berries.

Feuillette of Mixed Berries

Serves 8

8 oz.	*Puff Pastry (page 60)*
16 oz.	*whipped cream*
12 oz.	*fresh blueberries*
8 oz.	*fresh raspberries*
	powdered sugar for sprinkling
8 oz.	*Raspberry Sauce (page 55)*

THE *cellar* IN THE SKY

Chef's Canapés

Smoked Shrimp on Leek in Cream
and Sautéed Asparagus

Double Beef Consommé with Cheese Profiteroles

Pot au Feu with Salmon and Poivre Rose
— Sancerre, Château de Sancerre —

Roast Loin of Veal with Leek Confit
— Beaulieu Cabernet Sauvignon —

International Cheeseboard
— Châteauneuf-du-Pape, Paul Jaboulet Aîné —

Feuillette of Mixed Berries
— Schloss Vollrads Auslese —

Chocolate Truffles
Colombian Coffee

107th FLOOR/ONE WORLD TRADE CENTER/NEW YORK, N.Y. 10048/(212) 938-1111

(continued)

1 Roll the pastry till ⅛-inch thick; pierce with the tines of a fork and place on a large baking pan lined with parchment. Place another pan over it. Bake at 325°F until flaky and golden. Cool the dough and cut into sixteen 3-inch rounds.

2 *To assemble*: Place a puff pastry round on each dessert plate; put the whipped cream on the pastry. Strew with half the berries. Top with another round of puff pastry which has been sprinkled with powdered sugar. Surround with the raspberry sauce and the remaining berries. (You may also decorate with caramelized spun sugar as in the color photo, page H.)

PUFF PASTRY

Yields 1½ pounds

9 oz.	all-purpose flour
¾ oz.	sugar
dash	salt
8 oz.	lukewarm water
1¼ oz.	rum
8 oz.	unsalted butter
1 oz.	all-purpose flour

1 Mix the 9 oz. of flour, the sugar, and salt in a small bowl; add the water and rum. Knead on a marble or wooden surface to make a smooth dough.

2 Shape dough into a round form; cut crosswise on the top, but not all the way through. Cover with a clean kitchen towel and rest the dough for 1 hour.

3 Mix butter with the 1 oz. of flour; shape into a 2 × 2-inch brick. Set aside in refrigerator.

4 Roll out the dough evenly to all 4 sides. Put the butter-flour brick into the middle; fold dough over the butter brick so that it is completely covered.

5 Roll to about 1 inch thick. Fold the dough into thirds.

6 Roll out again, until dough is 1-inch thick. This time fold dough into quarters.

7 Cover dough with a towel and put in the refrigerator for 1 hour; then repeat steps 5 and 6.

8 Keep covered in refrigerator until needed. You can keep this puff pastry covered in the refrigerator for 3 to 5 days or frozen for 2 months.

9 To make fleurons, follow directions on page 89.

Dessert—the last course to be served in a meal—is quite important to a menu. A very good dessert can compensate for a mediocre main course, but a poor dessert can ruin the impression made by an excellent one. In the afternoon, on the other hand, a dessert can stand alone as a meal with a cup of coffee or tea. The sugar in the dessert helps rebuild your energy. Some desserts—such as cheese dumplings, strudels, or pancakes—can be served following a hearty soup to make a complete and substantial meal. Desserts have important significance on religious holidays, especially on Fridays when no meat is eaten.

Rosemount Chardonnay—Australia

One of the most sophisticated vineyard complexes in Australia, Rosemount produces top varietals such as Chardonnay, Pinot Noir, and Cabernet Sauvignon. This white wine is medium in body and the fruit of the Chardonnay grape goes together with the "sweetness" of the lobster meat.

Château Beychevelle—Bordeaux, France

This fourth-growth Bordeaux is considered by wine connoisseurs to be much better than its ranking. This wine, made primarily with the Cabernet Sauvignon grape variety, is a good choice with soft cheeses such as Brie, Camembert, and St. André. Look for the 1979 vintage.

Acacia Pinot Noir—Napa Valley, California

I have chosen the Acacia Pinot Noir, which I consider to be one of the top vineyards for the production of this varietal in California, because even when young, the essence of the Pinot Noir fruit matches the texture of the Sautéed Breast of Wild Duckling.

VINTAGE
1981

ACACIA
PINOT NOIR
NAPA VALLEY – CARNEROS DISTRICT
MADONNA VINEYARD

PRODUCED AND BOTTLED BY ACACIA WINERY
NAPA, CALIFORNIA. ALC. 13.5% BY VOL.

THE
cellar
IN THE SKY

Chef's Canapés
Salad of Sweetbreads with Wild Mushrooms
Bisque of Fennel with Saffron Quenelles
Feuilletage
with Lobster, Spinach and Small Vegetables
— Rosemount Chardonnay —
Sautéed Breast of Wild Duckling
with Braised Stuffed Leg and Poached Figs
— Acacia Pinot Noir —
International Cheeseboard
— Château Beychevelle —
Orange Tart with Bitter Chocolate Sorbet
— Château Rieussec —
Chocolate Truffles
Colombian Coffee

107th FLOOR/ONE WORLD TRADE CENTER/NEW YORK, N.Y. 10048//(212) 938-1111

Orange Tart with Bitter Chocolate Sorbet

Serves 4

Château Rieussec—Sauternes, France

Château Rieussec is one of the top Sauternes producers, and like most good Sauternes, it is very sweet but balanced. Look for 1975, 1976, 1979, and 1981 vintages.

4	*oranges*
24 oz.	*Simple Syrup (recipe follows)*
¼ recipe	*Puff Pastry (page 60)*
2 oz.	*powdered sugar*
7 oz.	*Pastry Cream (recipe follows)*
1 cup	*English Cream (recipe follows)*
½ recipe	*Orange Mousse (recipe follows)*
1 recipe	*Bitter Chocolate Sorbet (recipe follows)*

1 Peel the oranges; cut peels into 1½-inch-wide strips; divide the segments and reserve for the garnish. Remove the white membrane from the peels with a sharp knife. In a saucepan, bring the syrup to a boil; add the peel strips, lower the heat, and simmer over very low heat for 3 hours.

(continued)

English Cream

Serves 10 (2-ounce servings)

    8 oz. milk
    8 oz. heavy cream
      6 egg yolks
 3½ oz. sugar

1 Combine the milk and cream in a saucepan and bring to a boil.

2 In a bowl, whip the egg yolks and sugar until very foamy.

3 Stir the egg and sugar mixture into the milk and cream. Heat very slowly to 170°F, stirring constantly.

4 Set aside, occasionally removing the skin forming on the surface; strain before using. Store in the refrigerator.

2 Transfer peel slices to a wire rack to drain; the syrup should look like a very thick, almost dry, coating. Save syrup for another dish.

3 Roll the puff pastry to ⅛-inch thickness. Transfer pastry to a baking sheet lined with parchment; pierce pastry with tines of a fork. Place another baking sheet on top.

4 Bake in a preheated oven at 350°F for 8 to 10 minutes until golden brown; let cool.

5 Using a cooking cutter, cut the baked puff pastry into four 3-inch rounds.

6 Sprinkle powdered sugar on each round and place under a heated broiler for 3 to 4 seconds until the sugar melts to make a glaze.

7 Spread a little pastry cream on each glazed pastry round.

8 Arrange 6 glazed orange peel strips in a pyramid style on each pastry round.

9 Place the garnished tarts in a moderate oven for 5 to 6 minutes to warm throughout.

10 *To serve*: Arrange tarts on plates with English cream, a scoop of orange mousse, and a scoop of the chocolate sorbet. Also, garnish around the plate with the orange segments reserved from step 1. (Color photo on page H.)

PASTRY CREAM

Yields 20 ounces

      5 egg yolks
  16 oz. milk
   2 oz. cornstarch
   4 oz. sugar
      ½ vanilla bean

1 Mix egg yolks and 4 oz. (one-fourth) of the milk with the cornstarch.

2 Heat the remaining milk with the sugar and vanilla bean.

3 Slowly add the cold milk with the dissolved cornstarch and the egg yolks to the hot milk. Stirring constantly with a wooden spoon, bring to a boil. Set aside and let cool.

4 Store in the refrigerator, covered with plastic wrap.

BITTER CHOCOLATE SORBET

Serves 8

4 oz.	bitter chocolate
8 oz.	water
7 oz.	sugar
8 oz.	dry Champagne

1 Break chocolate into small pieces.

2 In a saucepan, bring water to a boil and add the sugar and chocolate, stirring until melted; let cool.

3 Stir in the Champagne. Freeze in the sorbet machine. Store sorbet in a freezer until needed.

ORANGE MOUSSE

Serves 10 (Yields 2 quarts)

6	gelatin leaves (or 1¾ oz. unflavored gelatin powder)
16 oz.	fresh orange juice
2 oz.	sugar
4½ oz.	egg whites
3½ oz.	powdered sugar
12 oz.	heavy cream

1 Soak 6 leaves of gelatin in cold water for 15 minutes.

2 Bring the orange juice to a boil in a saucepan; add the granulated sugar.

3 Remove from the heat and add the soaked gelatin leaves (only the leaves, not the water).

4 In a bowl, whip the egg whites, gradually adding the powdered sugar when half stiff. Continue to whip until stiff.

5 In another bowl, whip the heavy cream until stiff.

6 Fold the egg white mixture into the orange mixture. Then fold in the whipped cream.

7 Set aside in a stainless steel or plastic container until needed; or scoop into wine glasses, glass cups, or plates. Refrigerate until ready to serve.

If you want to make sorbet but do not have a sorbet machine: Pour the mixture into a flat bowl and put the bowl in a freezer. With a wire whisk, whip the sorbet every 30 minutes. Repeat these steps until it has the desired consistency. You may want to set your freezer to the coldest temperature for this period to increase the speed of freezing.

Simple Syrup

Yields 24 oz.

12 oz.	sugar
16 oz.	water

1 Mix the sugar and water in a saucepan; bring to a boil; cool before using.

When making simple syrup, prepare it ahead of time. Make sure it is in a bottle or jar with a tight cork or lid. In this way you can have the syrup handy whenever you may need it. Simple syrup can be used for sorbet, fruit sauce, and even for some cocktails.

Chablis-Valmur, Moreau—Burgundy, France

Valmur is one of the seven Grand Crus of Chablis, which means more alcohol, more body, and more Chardonnay flavor. With the Mousseline of Trout with Frog Legs, I want the most full-bodied of of the Chablis rather than a Village or Premier Cru, which might not be able to stand up to the mousseline. Moreau is one of the largest and best producers of Chablis. Look for the 1983 vintage.

Joseph Heitz Cabernet Sauvignon—Napa Valley, California

Heitz Vineyards produces one of the top-five Cabernet Sauvignons in all of California. Besides this particular wine, Heitz also makes a Heitz Cabernet Sauvignon—Martha's Vineyard, which needs more time to age but when mature could also go very well with the Medallions of Lamb. I usually recommend a Bordeaux or a high-quality California Cabernet because these wines blend nicely with the strong taste of lamb. Look for the 1980, 1981, and 1982 vintages.

Barbaresco, Gaja—Piedmont, Italy

Barbaresco and Barolo are considered two of the biggest red wines made in Italy. Both are made with the Nebbiolo grape variety and have high alcohol and tannin content. In many cases, these wines need ten to twenty years of aging. When young, they usually overpower many foods; therefore, this Barbaresco is put with the cheese course where the protein of the cheese softens the wine's high tannin content. Angelo Gaja recommends the 1978, 1979, and 1982 vintages.

THE
cellar
IN THE SKY

Chef's Canapés
Salad of Roast Pigeon with Antichokes and Wild Mushrooms
Cream of Savoy Cabbage with Truffles
Mousseline of Trout with Frog Legs
— Chablis-Valmur, Moreau —
Medallions of Lamb with Puréed Onion Gratin and Tomato Confit
— Joseph Heitz Cabernet Sauvignon —
International Cheeseboard
— Barbaresco, Gaja —
Apple Charlotte
— Château Climens —
Petits Fours
Colombian Coffee

107th FLOOR/ONE WORLD TRADE CENTER/NEW YORK, N.Y. 10048//(212) 938-1111

Château Climens—Barsac/Sauternes, France

After the famous and expensive Château d'Yquem, Château Climens is my favorite Sauternes. This wine, even in "off" vintages, displays a richness of fruit and balance of acidity. Look for the 1975, 1976, 1979, and 1981 vintages.

Apple Charlotte

Serves 8

	Apple-Layered Moulds (recipe follows)
4	McIntosh apples
3 oz.	unsalted butter
4 oz.	powdered sugar
2 oz.	applejack or Calvados
½	lemon, squeezed for the juice
5 oz.	Crème Fraîche (page 36)
1 oz.	powdered sugar
3 oz.	egg whites
1 oz.	granulated sugar
4	gelatin leaves or 1½ oz. unflavored gelatin
2 oz.	dry white wine
	fresh mint leaves for garnish
3 oz.	apricot jam or jelly, melted, for glaze
20 oz.	Mint Sorbet (recipe follows)
8	Hippen Shells (page 35)

1 Peel and core the apples; slice into eighths.

2 In a skillet, heat the butter and add the 4 oz. of powdered sugar. Lightly carmelize the sugar, add the apples and continue to carmelize over low heat. Deglaze with the applejack or Calvados and the lemon juice. In a processor, purée the apple mixture until smooth. Keep lukewarm.

(continued)

The Cellar
in the Sky

The Hors D'Oeuvrerie

The Restaurant

The Sushi and Seafood Bar
in the
Hors D'Oeuvrerie

K

(*clockwise from top left*)

Mushrooms à la Grecque

Pike and Bay Scallop Terrine

Salad of Feta, Olives,
   and Tomatoes

Orange and Onion Salad

Ceviche of Red Snapper

L

The Hors D'Oeuvrerie
(*clockwise from top left*)

Quiche Tartlets with Bacon and Chive

Marinated Salmon
   with Sour Cream Blinis

Boureks Stuffed with Sweetbreads
   and Mushrooms/Ground Lamb

Stuffed Pattypan Squash
   with Fresh Mussels

The Hors D'Oeuvrerie
(*clockwise from top left*)

Smoked Trout Fillet in Vegetable Aspic

Quail Galantine with Duck Liver

Tomato Barquette with
   Avocado Mousse and Truffle

Sea Scallop on Cucumber

Quail Egg on Marinated
   Baby Artichoke Heart

Dauphinoise Potatoes

Roast Loin of Veal
Filled with Spinach and Pignolias

Roast Beef Tenderloin
Stuffed with Morels

P

Duchesse Potatoes

3 In a bowl, whip the crème fraîche with the 1 oz. of powdered sugar until mixture has some firmness.

4 In another bowl, whip the egg whites with the granulated sugar until firm.

5 Soak the gelatin leaves or gelatin in the wine and dissolve by heating in the top of a double boiler. Then add the lukewarm apple purée.

6 Next, fold the crème fraîche mixture into the apple mixture; then fold in the egg white mixture.

7 Spoon the combined mixtures into the apple-layered moulds, spreading evenly on top.

8 Refrigerate the moulds for at least 4 to 6 hours; then turn the moulds upside down and unmould. Lightly brush the apple charlotte with the melted apricot glaze. Garnish with mint leaves.

9 *To assemble and serve*: Carefully place a scoop of mint sorbet in the hippen shells; arrange on the dessert plates with the apple charlotte. The color photo on page H shows a mirror aspic on a plate. To make this mirror aspic, use 3 leaves of gelatin or 1¼ oz. unflavored gelatin soaked in water and 10 oz. of clear, canned apple juice. Heat the apple juice in a saucepan and dilute gelatin in it. Slowly pour the juice onto a chilled plate with a flat surface. Refrigerate until the juice is jellied. Keep in a cool place until ready to serve. Then nicely arrange the apple charlotte and hippen shells filled with sorbet onto it.

Apple-Layered Moulds

> 3 McIntosh apples,
>   peeled and cored
> 16 oz. water
> 1 lemon, squeezed for
>   the juice
> 2 oz. applejack or Calvados
> 8 oz. granulated sugar

1 Cut the peeled and cored apples in half and then in slices.

2 In a saucepan, combine the water, lemon juice, applejack or Calvados and sugar; bring to a boil. Carefully place the sliced apples into the liquid. Do not boil; immediately remove from the heat and let the apples cool in the liquid.

3 Use the apples to line the forms or moulds.

4 Line up your available moulds, such as small cups, ramekins, or soufflé moulds; line moulds with the sliced apples and refrigerate until ready to fill.

Mint Sorbet

Serves 8

> 15 oz. water
> 7 oz. sugar
> 4 oz. fresh mint leaves
> 1 lemon, squeezed for
>   the juice

1 In a saucepan, bring water to a boil and stir in the sugar. Remove from heat. Set aside to cool.

2 Save some of the mint leaves for garnish; chop and stir the remaining mint into the syrup. Add the lemon juice.

3 Freeze the mixture in a sorbet machine till soft. Decorate with mint leaves and serve immediately or refreeze for later use.

The Hors D'Oeuvrerie

Long before the term "grazing" was used to describe the act of eating small samplings of a variety of foods, Windows on the World had a special section of the restaurant reserved for serving light fare and drinks called the Hors D'Oeuvrerie. Its menu is international, with special offerings featuring dishes from Brazil, Morocco, India, China, and Japan, to name only a few. The Hors D'Oeuvrerie had one of the first sushi bars in town—back when New Yorkers weren't so sure abut the idea of eating raw fish. They soon acquired a taste for it, and it caught on in such a big way that you can order sushi and sashimi there every day of the year.

The Hors D'Oeuvrerie is a relaxing place to unwind. Waiters and waitresses help set the casual mood by wearing colorful ethnic costumes, and a jazz trio tastefully plays background music in the evening. It's a place to talk while having drinks and appetizers. And you can visit it on the spur of the moment because reservations are not accepted.

The ways to enjoy the Hors D'Oeuvrerie are virtually endless. Some people prefer having a drink or sharing a bottle of wine, gazing at the sunset and spectacular view, overlooking the Brooklyn Bridge or the Statue of Liberty. Others may sample a few hors d'oeuvres as a light meal, or browse through the menu to concoct an interesting dinner.

Champagne and Sparkling Wine

When you think of special occasions and celebrations, Champagne is the drink that comes to mind before any other.

Actually, Champagne is a misunderstood wine in more ways than one. First of all, many people call practically anything that contains bubbles Champagne. *All Champagne is sparkling wine, but not all sparkling wine is Champagne.* Only sparkling wine produced in the French region of Champagne truly has a right to the name—and with good reason, I believe, because the Champagne area of France produces the best sparkling wine in the world. That's not to say that you should only drink Champagne, because there are some excellent-quality sparkling wines available made in the same way—the *Méthode Champenoise.* Some notable examples come from California and Spain.

The second misconception is that Champagne is meant to be served only on rare occasions, with hors d'oeuvres or wedding cake. Champagne is a wine that can enhance any or all of your dinner courses if you apply the same logic in selecting it that you use for any other wine. In fact, if you experiment with matching different Champagnes to various foods, you'll probably begin to realize that it is an unusually versatile wine. For instance, I only recently discovered that Champagne stands up to a strong cheese to make a surprisingly good combination. What a nice way to end a meal and then go on to dessert!

As with the other wines discussed so far, there is a difference in the tastes of Champagnes. It can be rated light-bodied, medium-bodied and full-bodied. One of the main factors that determines this is the way in which Champagne is fermented and aged. The lighter-style ones are aged in stainless steel, whereas many of the fuller ones spend more time aging in wood.

At the Hors D'Oeuvrerie, we serve many types of sushi and sashimi—among them:
Mirugai—orange shellfish
Tamago—egg
Hamachi—yellowtail
Maguro—tuna
Kappa maki—cucumber rolled in rice and dried seaweed
Tekka maki—tuna rolled in rice and dried seaweed
Futo maki—rice and vegetables rolled in dried seaweed
Ika—squid
Tako—octopus
Ebi—prawn
Nari maki (kanpyo)—dried gourd shavings rolled in rice and dried seaweed
Hirame—flounder
gary—vinegared ginger (used as a garnish)

Champagne makes a great apéritif. We use Champagne frequently at the Cellar in the Sky.

Some sparkling wines that I recommend are:
Codorniu—Spain
Freixenet—Spain
Henkell-Trocken—Germany
Domaine Chandon—California
Piper-Sonoma—California
Schramsberg—California
Korbel—California

Looking Over
Champagne's Body . . .

Light-Bodied	*Medium-Bodied*	*Full-Bodied*
Charbaut	Deutz	Bollinger
Laurent-Perrier	Moët & Chandon	Krug
Perrier-Jouët	Mumm	Roederer
Pol Roger	Pommery	Veuve Clicquot
Taittinger	Ruinart	
	Piper Heidsieck	

Dry Champagne has fewer calories than most table wines!

Now that you have some idea of a Champagne's body, you are ready to make your next decision: sweet or dry? Once again, there are levels of sweetness and dryness. Look on the bottle for one of the following labels to help you make a choice: "brut"—driest; "extra dry"—less dry; "sec"—more sweet; "demi-sec"—sweetest. One fact I've noticed at Windows on the World is that five out of ten of our customers who order Champagne have it served with dessert. Their selection is nearly always a brut style. My suggestion is to choose an extra-dry one, if you insist on having a dry Champagne, because you need a touch of sweetness for it to be compatible with cake.

Another factor you will undoubtedly consider when you choose a Champagne is price. Price is largely determined by the level or category of the Champagne. There are three levels of Champagne:

Non-vintage—a blend of different vintages or years of Champagne. As many as ten vintages can be mixed together to make a bottle of non-vintage Champagne.

Vintage—made from 100 percent of the year's harvest that is labelled on the bottle.

Luxury—made from the best grapes of the best vineyards, such as Dom Perignon.

Now I'll let you in on a little secret: Seventy-five percent of all Champagne is non-vintage and represents the best value. It's also a truer example of the Champagne producer's real style. Compared to the vintage and the luxury Champagnes, the non-vintage is lighter in style.

And if you've ever wondered, you can have Champagne throughout an entire meal. Champagne producers such as Veuve Clicquot regularly plan full-course dinners using Champagne exclusively. Here's an example of such a menu:

Veuve Clicquot Brut Yellow Label
Gruyère Cheese Flan

La Grand Dame
Caviar with Buckwheat Blini

Veuve Clicquot Gold Label 1978
Coho Salmon
with sweet red pepper butter sauce

Veuve Clicquot Rosé 1979
Noisettes of Lamb
with fresh tarragon

Veuve Clicquot Extra Dry
Poached Pear
with raspberry purée

When you want to incorporate Champagne into the main menu, just remember the following: "The heavier the style of food, the heavier the style of Champagne." Quite simply, a thick sirloin steak would go well with a Bollinger, whereas a fillet of trout might to better with a Taittinger. The best way to find your own preference is to try various combinations—not an unpleasant assignment.

"He is a bold man who first swallowed an oyster," said King James I of England in the seventeenth century.

Clams and oysters must be alive and fresh with tightly closed shells or else they cannot be eaten. Good-quality oysters have well-cupped shells. You can buy freshly shucked oysters and clams for soups, chowders, and stews. Sea scallops (large) and bay scallops (small) are usually available only shucked, too.

Oysters come from many sources:
Belon—Europe
Bluepoint—Long Island, New York
Olympia—Olympia Bay, Washington
Western—North America

Sauce Mignonette
Use this sauce for oysters and clams.
Serves 8
8 oz. malt vinegar
¾ oz white peppercorn, cracked
½ oz. shallot, peeled and finely chopped

1 Combine all the ingredients in a bowl or jar.

2 Store in the refrigerator.

Always use a wooden cutting board; the plastic ones ruin your knives and dull the blades. Never put a black-handled chef's knife in your dishwasher. Clean knives with a wet towel and dry immediately.

Curry Sauce

Serves 8

3 oz.	unsalted butter
1	onion, peeled and diced
1	apple, peeled and cored
1	ripe banana
½ oz.	tomato paste
1 oz.	spicy curry powder
16 oz.	White Chicken Stock (page 77)
3 oz.	dried shredded coconut
3 oz.	fresh pineapple pieces
	salt

1 In a casserole, heat the butter and saute the onion until transparent. Add the apple, banana, and tomato paste, sautéing briefly.

2 Stir the curry powder into the mixture; then pour in the chicken stock and add the coconut, pineapple, and a little salt.

3 Bring to a boil and cook about 20 minutes.

4 Blend the mixture in a blender.

5 Correct the seasonings. Serve hot.

Glass Blower's Herring

Serves 8

3	large salt herrings
2	small carrots, peeled and sliced
2	red onion, peeled and sliced
½ oz.	fresh ginger, peeled and thinly sliced
3 oz.	horseradish, peeled and thinly sliced
4 oz.	leek, cut lengthwise and thinly sliced
20	white peppercorns, crushed
10	whole allspice, crushed
¼ oz.	white mustard seed
½ qt.	water
6 oz.	white vinegar
5 oz.	sugar

1 Clean the herrings; cut off the fins and tails. Remove the first skin and rinse in cold water.

2 Cut in ¾-inch slices and soak for about 4 hours, depending on how salty the herrings are.

3 To make the marinade, in a saucepan, mix all the remaining ingredients except the white vinegar and sugar; bring to a boil. Set aside; then stir in the vinegar and sugar; let cool.

4 Place herrings in layers in a large glass jar, alternating with the cool marinade. Marinate overnight or for at least 12 hours in the refrigerator.

5 Serve cold on a leaf of lettuce, with pumpernickel or rye bread.

Coconut Shrimp

Serves 8

24	shrimps (16 to 20 shrimps per pound)
9 oz.	all-purpose flour
4	egg whites
5 oz.	beer
	salt
	white pepper, freshly ground
12 oz.	dried shredded coconut
	vegetable oil, for frying
	Curry Sauce (recipe follows)

1   Clean the shrimps, leaving the tails on; devein, cut, and butterfly the shrimps.

2   Mix the flour and beer in a bowl.

3   In another bowl, whip the egg whites and fold into the batter; season with salt and pepper.

4   Hold a shrimp by the tail, one at a time, and dip in the batter; remove and coat well with the shredded coconut.

5   Deep-fry at 325°F until golden brown.

6   Serve hot with the Curry Sauce.

Crab-Meat Fritters

Serves 8

1 lb.	lump crab meat
4 slices	white bread
3½ oz.	milk
2 oz.	unsalted butter
2	eggs
1 oz.	green bell pepper, chopped
1 oz.	red bell pepper, chopped
⅓ oz.	chive, chopped
dash	Tabasco sauce and Worcestershire sauce
	salt
	white pepper, freshly ground
2 oz.	vegetable oil
6 oz.	Red Cocktail Sauce (recipe follows)

1   Cut the crab meat into even pieces. Place in a bowl.

2   Soak the bread in the milk in another bowl; squeeze out excess moisture. Add the soaked bread to the crab meat

3   In a bowl, whip the butter until fluffy; add the eggs, whipping constantly.

4   Blanch the green and red peppers in boiling water for a few seconds; drain and cool.

5   Add the blanched peppers to the crab meat and mix all the ingredients together. Season to taste with Tabasco and Worcestershire sauces, salt, and pepper. Using your fingers, shape the mixture into small patties.

6   Heat the vegetable oil in a skillet. Fry the patties until golden brown on both sides.

7   Serve the patties hot with the Red Cocktail Sauce on the side.

Red Cocktail Sauce

Serves 8

6 oz.	tomato ketchup
4 oz.	mild chili sauce
1 oz.	horseradish, freshly grated and finely chopped
¼ oz.	wine vinegar Worcestershire sauce
½	lemon, squeezed for the juice
dash	Tabasco sauce
	salt (optional)

1   In a bowl, combine all the ingredients and mix well. Correct the seasonings, if needed.

2   Refrigerate in a covered glass jar.

Keep all shellfish very chilled on ice, but not in cold water. Use a double-bottomed container so that the water can run out as the ice melts. Lobsters should be kept refrigerated in a container. Cover them with a wet towel (or wet newspaper) to keep them completely in the dark.

Chinese Lemon Spareribs

Serves 8

3 lbs.	spareribs	2 oz.	all-purpose flour
1 oz.	salt	4	egg whites
¼ oz.	white pepper, freshly ground	2 oz.	cold water
		8 oz.	vegetable oil for frying
2	lemons, squeezed for the juice	1	lemon rind, finely cut in julienne slices, blanched, and drained
2 oz.	soy sauce		
3 oz.	sesame oil		Pickled Cucumbers
¼ oz.	fresh ginger		(recipe follows)
2 oz.	cornstarch		

1 Trim the spareribs of excess fat; cut spareribs lengthwise; then cut in half through the bone.

2 In a bowl, make a marinade with the lemon juice, soy sauce, sesame oil, and ginger; marinate the ribs in the mixture for about 4 hours.

3 In another bowl, mix the cornstarch, flour, egg whites, and water to make a batter.

4 Heat the oil to 275°F in a deep skillet.

5 Dip spareribs into the batter and slowly fry them in the hot oil. Use a skimmer to remove from the skillet. Set on a paper towel to drain.

6 When serving, sprinkle with the blanched lemon rind. Serve with Pickled Cucumbers.

Guacamole

Serves 8

2	ripe avocados	1	garlic clove, finely chopped
1	tomato, diced		salt
¼ oz.	cilantro (fresh coriander), chopped		white pepper, freshly ground
⅛ oz.	lemon juice		

Tabasco sauce

1 Peel the avocados and discard the pits. In a bowl or blender, mash the avocado; add all the remaining ingredients.

2 Mix well and let stand for half an hour. Correct the seasonings.

3 Serve with tostados, tortilla chips, soda biscuits, or use instead of herbed butter on your charcoal-broiled steak.

Sesame: An annual herbaceous plant. The seeds yield a bland oil of a fine quality with a long shelf life.

Pickled Cucumbers

2 lbs. hothouse cucumbers
6 oz. rice wine vinegar
2 oz. sugar
dash cayenne pepper
3 oz. water
⅛ oz. salt

1 Leave the skins on the cucumbers. Cut off the ends; cut in half lengthwise and remove the seeds with a small spoon. Cut into 2-inch-long strips.

2 Make a marinade with the rice wine vinegar, sugar, cayenne pepper, water, and salt.

3 Place cucumber strips in the marinade. Marinate for 6 hours.

Coriander: An annual plant of the carrot family. The seeds have a strong smell used in cookery. Fresh coriander or cilantro is also fragrant and useful in cooking and as a garnish.

Barbecued Short Ribs of Beef

Serves 8

4 (1 lb. each)	beef short ribs
	salt
6 oz.	water
8 oz.	White Beef Stock (page 74, optional)
	soy sauce
3 oz.	sugar
½ oz.	garlic, chopped
½ oz.	fresh ginger, thinly sliced
2 oz.	scallion (white part only), diced
¹⁄₁₆ oz.	fresh chili pepper, finely chopped
6 oz.	Chinese rice wine
2 oz.	sesame oil
2 oz.	cornstarch
	Pickled Chinese Cabbage (recipe follows)

1 Trim the short ribs of excess fat; cut short ribs in half (ask your butcher to cut them across the bone).

2 Blanch short ribs in salted water or in the beef stock for about 2 minutes; drain.

3 In a bowl, make a marinade with all the remaining ingredients except the cornstarch. Immerse the warm short ribs in the marinade and make sure that all the ribs are covered.

4 Marinate for about 24 hours in the refrigerator.

5 Remove short ribs from the marinade. Slowly broil them, turning occasionally, using outdoor barbecue grill or an electric broiler; or set short ribs in a roasting pan and roast in an oven at 350°F for about 25 minutes. Baste the short ribs several times with the marinade while cooking.

6 In a saucepan, bring the marinade to a boil. In a cup, dilute the cornstarch in a little water, and stir into the marinade to thicken. Boil the sauce for half a minute.

7 Dress the short ribs on a plate and ladle some sauce on top. Serve with Pickled Chinese Cabbage.

Ginger: The root of a herbaceous perennial plant grown in most tropical countries.

Pickled Chinese Cabbage

Serves 8

2 lbs.	Chinese cabbage
5 oz.	rice wine vinegar
3 oz.	sugar
1	fresh hot chili, chopped
¹⁄₁₆ oz.	white pepper, freshly ground
⅛ oz.	salt
⅛ oz.	sesame seed
1	green bell pepper

1 Cut cabbage in 1-inch-square pieces; wash, rinse, and dry thoroughly. All leaves should be loose.

2 In a bowl, make a marinade with the vinegar, sugar, chili, salt, pepper, and sesame seed.

3 Dice the green pepper in ¼-inch pieces.

4 Fill a large pot with water and bring to a boil; add the salt. Drop the cabbage and green pepper into the water for 5 seconds; drain immediately.

5 Immerse the cabbage and green pepper in the marinade for about 6 hours in the refrigerator. Use a skimmer to lift the cabbage you need. Serve cold.

Grilled Fresh Chorizo with Black Beans

Serves 10

White Beef Stock

Yields 2 quarts

4 lbs.	beef bones, chopped 1-inch thick
8 qts.	water
	salt
4	bay leaves
10	white peppercorns
6 oz.	carrot
4 oz.	leek
4 oz.	celery
6 oz.	unpeeled onions, cut in half
3	soft tomatoes
1	fresh thyme sprig
1 bunch	parsley stems

1 Wash the bones thoroughly with hot water; then rinse with cold water.

2 Place in a large stockpot with the cold water. Slowly bring to a boil. Drain off the liquid. Rinse the bones in hot water and then in cold water.

3 Put bones back into the stockpot and fill with cold water. Slowly bring to a boil. Skim off the foam and fat. Add salt, bay leaves, and peppercorns.

4 Slowly simmer for about 1½ hours. Add all the vegetables. Cook for 45 minutes. Strain through a Chinese strainer set over a bowl.

5 Pour strained stock into the stockpot. Slowly simmer until the liquid is reduced to about 2 quarts.

6 Strain stock and cool. Skim off all the fat. Keep stock in the refrigerator to use within 3 days; or freeze in small plastic containers.

16 oz.	black beans
3 oz.	smoked bacon, diced
3 oz.	onion, diced
1 qt.	White Beef Stock (recipe follows)
	bouquet garni (1 sprig fresh parsley and fresh thyme, and a bay leaf)
3 tsp.	salt
½ tsp.	white pepper, freshly ground
dash	Tabasco sauce
3 oz.	green bell pepper, cut in julienne slices, blanched
3 oz.	red bell pepper, cut in julienne slices, blanched
6 oz.	onion rings
½ oz.	all-purpose flour
½ oz.	paprika
12 oz.	vegetable oil
	Fresh Chorizo (recipe follows)
½ oz.	fresh coriander (cilantro) leaves

1 Wash the beans and soak overnight.

2 Fry the bacon in a casserole; add the diced onions and sauté until onions are soft.

3 Drain the soaked beans and add to the casserole with half of the beef stock. Bring to a boil and add the bouquet garni. Lower the heat and simmer until the beans are tender, adding more beef stock, if necessary. Remove the bouquet garni. Season the beans with salt, white pepper, and Tabasco sauce.

4 Blanch the green and red peppers in boiling, salted water; drain.

5 Dust the onion rings with the flour and paprika and mix well. Heat the oil in a deep fryer and fry the onion rings until crispy.

6 Charcoal-broil the chorizos until done.

7 To assemble, dress the beans on plates. Place the chorizos on top of the beans. Garnish the plates with onion rings, red and green peppers, and coriander.

40 oz.	lean pork	dash	ground cumin
28 oz.	pork fat (50% fat)	dash	garlic powder
	salt	dash	onion powder
1/8 oz.	Spanish paprika	1/2 oz.	vinegar
1/16 oz.	ground black pepper	1/2 oz.	cilantro (fresh
dash	cayenne pepper		coriander), chopped

1 bundle　hog casing,
rinsed
and drained

1　Grind half of each amount of pork and pork fat, one through a fine (no. 1) blade, and the other through a coarse (no. 3) blade. Combine the ground pork and pork fat in a bowl.

2　Add all the seasonings and mix, using the dough hook, for about 3 minutes. Fill the casing, using a sausage-filling machine.

3　Form into 16 or 20 long chorizos by twisting the casing to the desired size. Store in the refrigerator and use within a day; or freeze. (If you don't have a machine, form by hand without the casing.)

Sate　　　　　　　　　　　　　　　　　**Serves 8**

5	shallots, peeled
2	garlic cloves, peeled
4	fresh lemon grass stalks or a handful of dried lemon grass blades
1/8 oz.	ground cumin
1/16 oz.	ground turmeric
1/8 oz.	tamarind paste
1/8 oz.	shrimp paste
1/8 oz.	salt
2 oz.	Japanese soy sauce (sweet)
pinch	black pepper, freshly ground
2 lbs.	beef, chicken, lamb, or pork, cut in small cubes
3 oz.	peanut oil

1　Finely chop the shallots, garlic, and lemon grass. Place in a bowl.

2　Add the cumin, turmeric, tamarind, shrimp paste, salt, soy sauce, and pepper and mix well.

3　Marinate the meat in the mixture overnight.

4　Soak wooden skewers in water for at least 20 minutes. Skewer the marinated meat or seafood.

5　Cook over charcoal, turning and basting frequently with peanut oil.

Cumin: An annual umbelliferous plant found wild in Syria and Egypt. An agreeable aromatic seed used in curries.

Japanese Noodle Salad

Serves 8

1 lb.	Japanese udon noodles salt to taste
1 oz.	soy sauce
1 oz.	sesame oil
1 oz.	rice wine vinegar
3 oz.	fresh, sliced shiitake mushrooms or 1 oz. dried Japanese mushrooms, soaked and sliced
1 oz.	scallion, sliced
1/4 oz.	hot pepper
1/2 oz.	red bell pepper, sliced
1/2 oz.	cilantro (fresh coriander) white pepper, freshly ground

1　In a large pot, cook the noodles in boiling salted water, keeping them firm. Drain, but do not freshen them with cold water.

2　Mix noodles with the soy sauce, sesame oil, and vinegar.

3　Spread the noodles on a tray to cool.

4　Then mix noodles in a bowl with the mushrooms, scallion, hot pepper, and red bell pepper.

5　Taste and season with white pepper and more hot pepper, if you wish.

Hacked Chicken

Serves 8

> 2   double breasts of boneless chicken, poached
> 1 qt.   White Chicken Stock (page 77)
>   Peanut and Sesame Sauce (recipe follows)
> 8 oz.   agar-agar
> ½ oz.   cilantro (fresh coriander) leaves

1   Poach chicken breasts in the chicken stock for about 12 minutes until the chicken is very tender.

2   In a bowl, mix all the ingredients for the sauce very well; set aside till ready to serve.

3   Soak the agar-agar in water for 10 minutes; drain and squeeze out the water.

4   Cut chicken into large julienne slices. Dress chicken on top of agar-agar. Ladle sauce generously on top and garnish with the cilantro leaves.

Vegetable Pakora

Serves 20 (2 per person)

> 24 oz.   chick-pea flour
> 1/16 oz.   salt
> 12 oz.   water
> 2   medium onions
> 1   medium eggplant
> 1   Idaho potato
> 1   medium zucchini
> ⅛ oz.   ground coriander
> ¼ oz.   ground cumin
> 1/16 oz.   ground turmeric
> 6   green chilies, seeded and chopped
> 1/16 oz.   garam masala (mixed spices available at Asian-Indian shops)
> 2   garlic cloves
> ⅛ oz.   fresh ginger, chopped
> 24 oz.   vegetable oil for frying

1   In a bowl, combine the chick-pea flour, salt, and water; the mixture should be thick. Let it stand for 5 to 10 minutes.

2   Slice the onion, eggplant, potato, and zucchini in julienne slices.

3   Mix the vegetables with the spices and seasonings; combine with the batter.

Peanut and Sesame Sauce

> 6 oz.   peanut butter
> 6 oz.   sesame paste or tahini
> 3 oz.   sugar
> 2 oz.   sesame oil
> 3 oz.   soy sauce
> dash   Chinese hot sauce or Tabasco sauce
> 1 oz.   white vinegar
> ½ oz.   cilantro (fresh coriander)

1   In a bowl, combine all the ingredients and mix well. Store in a covered jar in the refrigerator.

Garlic: A plant of the lily family. Garlic cloves are used to flavor a variety of dishes, including meats and salads.

4   Pour the oil into a deep fryer. Heat to 350°F; drop the vegetable-batter mixture, a teaspoon at a time, into the hot oil; fry and turn the pakora. Continue frying pakora until golden brown, draining them on paper towels. Arrange on a platter and serve warm or room temperature.

Vegetarian Samosa

Serves 16 (2 Samosas per person)

for FILLING

3 oz.	olive oil
1	medium onion, diced
1	garlic clove, chopped
1/16 oz.	fresh ginger, finely chopped
1/8 oz.	cumin seed, roasted
1/8 oz.	ground coriander
1/8 oz.	ground turmeric
	salt
6	green chilies, chopped
4 oz.	water
24 oz.	vegetable oil for frying

for DOUGH

24 oz.	all-purpose flour
	salt
4 oz.	unsalted butter, melted
8 oz.	water

1   Heat the oil in a skillet. Add the onion, garlic, and ginger; sauté until golden.

2   Add the spices, chilies, and water. Cook until the liquid has almost evaporated.

3   Add the potatoes and green peas; cook for 5 to 7 minutes until the filling looks dry; let cool.

4   To make the dough, mix the flour, salt, and butter in a stainless steel bowl. Add enough water to form a smooth dough that is firm but pliable; let rest.

5   Divide the dough into twenty 1-inch balls. Roll each ball into a circle approximately 6 inches in diameter. Cut each circle in half; each dough circle makes 2 samosas.

6   Place a teaspoon of filling on each dough semicircle; fold over into a triangle shape and press edges together with a fork.

7   Deep-fry the samosas until golden brown. Drain on paper towels. Serve hot. Heat the oil in a deep fryer.

Use this stock for white chicken sauce or chicken soup.

White Chicken Stock

Yields 2 quarts

3 lbs.	chicken backs, bones, wings, and necks, chopped into 1-inch pieces
4 qts.	cold water
3 oz.	onion, chopped
4 oz.	carrot, chopped
4 oz.	leek, washed and sliced
4 oz.	celery
2 oz.	mushroom stems
1	fresh thyme sprig
1	fresh parsley sprig
1	bay leaf
15	white peppercorns
1/2 oz.	salt

1   Wash the chicken in hot water to remove the blood.

2   Place the bones in a 5-quart stockpot, add the water and very slowly bring to a boil over a low burner. Skim off the foam and fat as they rise to the surface to make a clear stock.

3   Add the vegetables, herbs, and spices. Simmer for 45 minutes.

4   Set a Chinese strainer over a large pot or casserole and strain the stock. Skim off all the fat from the surface, or cool the stock and refrigerate; then discard the fat, using a slotted spoon (the fat will congeal when chilled).

5   Set pot with the stock over low heat and very slowly bring to the boiling point. Reduce heat and simmer gently until reduced to 2 quarts. Cool.

6   Refrigerate and use within 3 to 5 days; or freeze in 2-cup quantities for up to 3 months.

Kefta Kebab

2½ lbs.	ground lamb and/or ground beef
3 oz.	onion, grated
2	garlic cloves, crushed
½ oz.	cilantro (fresh coriander), chopped
½ oz.	fresh flat-leaf parsley, chopped
1/16 oz.	ground cumin
¼ oz.	Spanish or Hungarian paprika
dash	cayenne pepper
	salt
	black pepper, freshly ground
6 oz.	vegetable oil
	Harissa Sauce (recipe follows)

1 Grind the lamb through the no. 2 blade of a meat grinder (not too fine).

2 Add all the onion, garlic, herbs, and spices to the ground lamb, mixing well by hand. Let the mixture stand for 1 hour to marinate. Correct the seasoning, if necessary.

3 Divide mixture into 24 parts. Shape into 2 oz. slim, oval sausages. Thread each sausage onto a wooden skewer.

4 Grill on charcoal or an electric broiler for about 10 minutes. Do not overcook.

5 Serve with Harissa Sauce and warm pita bread. Arrange 3 kebabs per person on heated plates.

Scallion Pancakes

3 lbs.	all-purpose flour
1½ cups	cold water
	vegetable oil
4 oz.	melted beef kidney fat, soft butter, or vegetable oil
1 oz.	salt
½ oz.	white pepper, freshly ground
4	scallions, cut in ¼-inch dice
	Dumpling Sauce (recipe follows)

1 In a large bowl, mix the flour and water to form a stiff dough. Shape dough into a square, cover and set aside for 30 minutes.

2 Cut dough into 2 pieces. Cover one piece until ready to use.

You will need 24 5-inch wooden skewers to prepare this recipe.

Harissa Sauce

Serves 8

4 oz.	red chili paste (sambal oelek) (available at Hispanic, Asian-Indian, and Indonesian shops)
1/16 oz.	ground cumin
½	garlic clove, finely crushed
3 oz.	olive oil
½ oz.	onion, chopped
	salt to taste
1/16 oz.	fresh coriander (cilantro), chopped

1 In a bowl, combine all the ingredients except the oil. Mix well by hand. (Do not use a food processor or blender.) Add the oil and blend well.

2 Store in the refrigerator till ready to use.

3 Coat a pastry board with the oil and roll the dough into an oblong, 30 inches long and ¼ thick; turn the dough 4 times as you roll it.

4 Spread half the fat; butter, or oil over the dough, covering completely. Sprinkle half the salt and pepper over the dough, pressing the spices into the dough. Sprinkle with half of the diced scallions, covering the dough completely.

5 Starting from the edge nearest you, roll up as a jelly roll. Press the edge of the dough to seal. Cut roll into 5 equal pieces. Repeat with the other half of the dough.

6 Pinch the open edge of each piece to seal and form a dumpling: then press your finger into the closed end to make a dimple in the middle of the dumpling.

7 Pour the vegetable oil ¼-inch deep into a pan. Place the dumplings in the pan and set aside to rest for a few minutes.

8 Remove the dumplings, place them on a flat surface, and punch down. Keeping your hand well oiled, press out from the middle and shape into 7-inch rounds. Let the pancakes rest for a few minutes.

9 Heat enough oil to cover ¼ inch of the bottom of a large skillet. Fry the pancakes until golden brown on each side.

10 Drain pancakes on a rack to remove excess oil.

11 Serve hot, whole or cut into sections, with Dumpling Sauce.

Mousse of Duck Liver

Serves 6 to 8

8 oz.   *dry white wine, such as a Riesling*
½ lb.   *fresh duck liver, cleaned and drained*
½ lb.   *unsalted butter, at room temperature*
1 oz.   *Madeira*
1 oz.   *Port*
        salt and freshly ground white pepper to taste

1 In a saucepan, bring the white wine to a boil; add the liver and simmer for 3 minutes. Drain off the wine; cool the liver.

2 Combine the liver and all remaining ingredients in a food processor. Blend with a sharp blade for 1 to 2 minutes until it has the consistency of a mousse paste. Remove from the processor and refrigerate.

3 Serve cold as an appetizer, hors d'oeuvre, or a canapé on toast.

Dumpling Sauce

16 oz. *soy sauce*
¼ oz.   *white pepper, freshly ground*
½ oz.   *sugar*
½ oz.   *sesame oil*
1½ oz. *Worcestershire sauce*
1 oz.   *oyster sauce*
¾ oz.   *chili paste with garlic (available in oriental shops)*
4 oz.   *cold water*
1   *scallion, cleaned and cut into ¼-inch dice*

1 In a bowl, combine all the ingredients thoroughly. Taste to check the seasoning. Store in a covered jar in the refrigerator.

2 Serve with Scallion Pancakes.

1983
Chateau St. Jean
ALEXANDER VALLEY
Johannisberg Riesling
(White Riesling)
Special Select Late Harvest
ROBERT YOUNG VINEYARDS
PRODUCED AND BOTTLED BY
CHATEAU ST. JEAN • KENWOOD, SONOMA VALLEY, CALIFORNIA, USA
BONDED WINERY NO. 4710 • ALCOHOL 8.2% BY VOLUME

The Restaurant

The main dining room at Windows on the World is called the Restaurant, and it has the largest seating capacity of all the dining areas. The Restaurant caters to a very broad, international clientele. Its popularity is attributed to careful planning and keeping abreast of current marketing trends. The menu is a culinary extravaganza, filled with dishes that are sure to please everyone, no matter how diverse the party. From the beginning, the menu was designed not only with taste and variety in mind, but with price and value.

The very first menu offered a selection of à la carte items on one side and a full prix fixe menu on the other. This concept remains the same today, even though the individual selections have become lighter in texture and taste. The menu undergoes three major changes each year to reflect seasonal changes and availability of food. Director Alan Lewis said, "We don't serve chicken livers with blueberries anymore, but there're still some interesting combinations on the menu."

At all times at the Restaurant, guests can select any one of 700 wines from around the world that are available on the regular and extended wine lists, which are the largest in New York City, and they are very reasonably priced.

The Restaurant is masterfully designed with multi-leveled tiers and clever use of mirrors to enable all customers to admire the panoramic view. All in all, it is a restaurant ideal for any type of celebration. People plan ahead and make reservations to dine there. They look forward to the whole experience, which is enhanced by the outstanding service from the staff. As President Anton Aigner said, "It is a team effort here. It's not a one-man show, but a combination of individual efforts."

Wines for Buffet Dining

Picture yourself at a beautifully arranged buffet table—with dishes ranging from soup to nuts. As you progress down the length of the table, you make various selections. Once you've decided how to strategically fit everything onto your undersized plate, you are faced with the even more difficult task of choosing one wine that matches well with your festive dish.

You're probably about to taste some distinct and exotic spices, vinegar in salads, and assorted fruits and cheeses—all at the

Anton Aigner

Alan Lewis

same time! What should you drink? Try a glass of Champagne or sparkling wine. The carbonation cuts through the strong spices and it doesn't overpower most foods.

But maybe you prefer a wine without the carbon dioxide. The following inexpensive and medium-priced wine lists offer red and white wines that you can serve at a buffet. Remember, there's no need to spend an outrageous amount of money on wine.

If you find yourself a little low on money after buying all of the ingredients for your feast, I would recommend the following inexpensive jug wines. Many people turn up their noses at the thought of an *ordinary* jug wine, but the brands from California are among the best-made drinking wines (not sipping) in the world. There are also some very good table wines from France that will go nicely with a buffet. If the jug wines don't suit you, and you prefer to offer more upscale wines without spending a lot of money, check the medium-priced wine list.

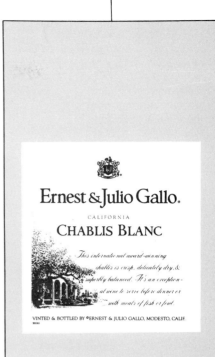

The Inexpensive Wine List
Almaden
Gallo
Inglenook
Paul Masson
Robert Mondavi
   (red/white table wine)
Monterey
Partager
Valbon
Chantefleur

The Medium-priced Wine List
Beaujolais
Chablis
Mâcon
Montagny
Rully
Soave
Bardolino
Pinot Grigio
White Zinfandel
   ("Blush" wines)
German Kabinett

If you prefer something sweeter, try one of the German Spätleses. The extra sweetness can help to offset the acidity often found in the many salads of a buffet.

Mushrooms à la Grecque

Serves 8

32 oz.	water
⅛ oz.	fennel seed
⅛ oz.	coriander seed
⅛ oz.	dried thyme
1	bay leaf
10	black peppercorns
2 lbs.	small firm mushrooms
2 oz.	vegetable oil
2 oz.	olive oil
3	lemons, squeezed for the juice
	salt to taste

1 Bring water to a boil; add the fennel and coriander seed, thyme, bay leaf, and peppercorns. Simmer for about 20 minutes; strain the marinade into a bowl.

2 Wash the mushrooms; if too large, cut into quarters or halves.

3 Heat the combined oils in a casserole; add the mushrooms and sauté lightly. Stir in the lemon juice and salt. Add the marinade and simmer for about 12 minutes.

4 Let mushrooms cool in the marinade. Serve well chilled. (Color photo on page L.)

Orange and Onion Salad

Serves 8

2	bunches watercress, stems removed
6	oranges, segmented and membranes removed
1	medium red onion, thinly sliced
2 oz.	black cured olives, pitted
	Cumin Dressing (recipe follows)

1 Make a nest of watercress in a serving bowl.

2 Combine the orange sections, onion, and olives. Add the dressing and mix well.

3 Arrange the salad in the middle of the watercress nest. Serve cold. (Color photo on page L.)

"It is easy to refrain from gold, silver, and the joy of love, but it is difficult to refrain from a tasty mushroom dish!"
Marcus Valerian Martial, the Roman philosopher, *First century A.D.*

Serve Mushrooms à la Grecque for a buffet salad or as an hors d'oeuvre. You can use the same marinade for artichoke hearts, fennel, pearl onions, squash, cauliflower, carrots, and leeks. Just adjust the cooking time accordingly.

Cumin Dressing

4 oz.	olive oil
⅛ oz.	ground cumin
2 oz.	orange juice
	salt
½	garlic clove, chopped
½ oz.	white vinegar

1 Combine all the ingredients in a jar and shake well.

2 Refrigerate until ready to use.

Saffron Onions

Serves 4

4 oz.	white raisins
12 oz.	dry white wine
32 oz.	frozen small white onions
4 oz.	olive oil
1	fresh tomato, peeled, seeded and chopped
1/32 oz.	saffron
	salt
	white pepper, freshly ground

1 Wash the raisins; place in a bowl, add the wine, and soak the raisins for 2 or more hours. Drain, reserving the wine.

2 Blanch the onions in salted water for half a minute and drain.

3 Sauté the onions in olive oil with the tomato and raisins for half a minute. Add the reserved wine, saffron, salt, and pepper; simmer gently for 20 minutes. Serve at room temperature.

Salad of Green Beans and New Potatoes in Aquavit Dressing

Serves 8

2 lbs.	tiny green beans, cleaned
1/2 lb.	new potatoes
	salt
6	bacon slices
5 oz.	walnut oil
1/16 oz.	ground caraway seed
1/2 oz.	aquavit

1 Cook the beans in boiling salted water until just tender. Drain and refresh in cold water.

2 Boil the unpeeled potatoes in salted water until just done. Drain and refresh in cold water. Quarter the potatoes.

3 Fry the bacon until crisp. Drain and chop finely.

4 Mix the oil, caraway seed, and aquavit to make the dressing.

5 Combine the beans, potatoes, and bacon in a large bowl and toss with the dressing. Serve warm.

Saffron: The stigma of the Crocus sativus. It is dried and used to flavor stocks, meats, fish, and other dishes. Saffron has an orange-red hue.

When boiling potatoes in their skins for salad, use enough salt, a dash of caraway seed, a piece of butter, a sprig of dill and parsley (or the stem). If there is not enough salt, even if you add salt afterwards, the potatoes will taste plain. You will want to eat the potatoes while you peel them. So delicious a boiled potato can be.

When buying oil for salad, buy good-quality olive oil. When using walnut oil or hazelnut oil in salad dressing, never use it alone; mix at least half with good vegetable oil or olive oil. Walnut and hazelnut oils have such a strong taste, they overpower the flavor of the lettuce.

Salad of Feta, Olives, and Tomatoes

Serves 8

1 lb.	feta, cut in cubes
½ lb.	onion, sliced in rings
4	large tomatoes, cut in cubes
3	large green bell peppers, sliced in rings
24	Greek wrinkled or Nicoise black olives, pitted
2 oz.	olive oil
1½ oz.	vinegar
1	garlic clove, crushed o. minced
	ground cumin to taste
	black pepper, freshly ground, to taste

1 Place the feta, onion, tomatoes, peppers, and olives in a serving bowl.

2 To make the dressing, mix together the oil, vinegar, garlic, cumin, and pepper. Pour over the vegetable-feta mixture; toss. Serve cold.

White Bean and Tuna Salad

Serves 8

8 oz.	small white navy beans
2	garlic cloves
4 oz.	olive oil
⅛ oz.	wine vinegar
	salt
	white pepper, freshly ground
3¼ oz.	canned flaked tuna
1	fresh parsley sprig, chopped, for garnish

1 Soak the beans in water overnight. Rinse and cook according to package directions; or simmer for 1¼ hours in boiling salted water until just tender. Drain and cool the beans in a bowl.

2 Mince the garlic and sauté briefly in the oil in a skillet. Pour the garlic and oil over the beans and toss.

3 Mix together the vinegar, salt, pepper, and tuna. Toss with the beans and refrigerate.

4 Garnish with the parsley before serving. Serve cold.

Some of our hot buffet dishes at Windows on the World include:
  Curried Chicken
  Chicken in Red Wine Sauce
  Lamb Navarin in Vegetables and Tomatoes
  Seafood Paella with Shrimp, Clams, and Mussels
  Beef Stew in Red Wine Sauce
  Beef and Kidney Pie
  Pot Roast with Pearl Onions and Tiny Mushrooms
  Stuffed Breast of Veal with Spinach and Pignolia
  Roast Leg of Lamb with Olives and Anchovies
  Roast Pork Loin Stuffed with Prunes
  Marinated Roast Beef Tenderloin
  Coca-Cola-Glazed Cured Ham
  Seafood Jambalaya
  Arroz con Pollo
  Seafood Creole
  Tortellini alla Panna
  Boiled Brisket of Beef
  Corned Beef and Pastrami
  Sauerkraut with German Sausages and Smoked Pork Loin
  Cassolette of Duck, Pork, and Sausage

Turkey and Apple Salad

Serves 8

3	Golden Delicious apples
½	lemon, squeezed for the juice
	salt
	white pepper, freshly ground
1 lb.	cooked turkey breast, cut in ¾-inch cubes
4 oz.	mayonnaise
3 oz.	walnut halves

1 Core the apples, and cut in ¾-inch cubes, sprinkling with 2 tablespoons of the lemon juice to prevent discoloration.

2 In a bowl, mix together the remaining lemon juice, salt, and pepper. Toss with the turkey. Add the apples and mayonnaise and toss again.

3 Sprinkle walnut halves over the top before serving. Serve cold.

In your creative recipes, try to cut down on salt and pepper. Use sauces, fillings, or stuffings with some fresh herbs, coarsely chopped. Add herbs nearly at the end, when the dish is ready to be served. Then you will keep the original flavor of the herbs.

Fish Hash

Serves 8

1½ lbs.	cooked lean white fish
2	celery stalks, diced
½	onion, diced
1	lemon, squeezed for the juice
	salt
4 oz.	mayonnaise
2	lemons, thinly sliced
⅛ oz.	fresh parsley, chopped
	white pepper, freshly ground

1 Flake the fish with your fingers, separating into shreds and removing any bones or skin.

2 Place the shredded fish in a bowl. Add the celery, onion, salt, and lemon juice and toss. Add the mayonnaise and toss again.

3 Garnish with the lemon slices and parsley.

You may begin with 1½ lbs. of fish fillets or with 3½ lbs. of fish trimmings. To cook, poach the fish in boiling water flavored with salt to taste and freshly ground pepper, 1 bay leaf, ½ onion, chopped, and 1 stalk of celery, chopped. Poach for 10 minutes per inch of thickness of the fish. Drain and chill before shredding the fish. Serve cold.

Gravlax

Serves 8

1	side of fresh salmon	1	bay leaf
	(from a 4-lb. salmon),	$\frac{1}{16}$ oz.	dried sage
	skin on	$\frac{1}{16}$ oz.	dried marjoram
1 oz.	fresh dill	$\frac{1}{16}$ oz.	dried basil leaves
1 oz.	fresh parsley	$\frac{1}{2}$	fresh fennel root
1	carrot	2	garlic cloves
3 oz.	leek	6 oz.	salt
2 oz.	celery	9 oz.	sugar
$\frac{1}{16}$ oz.	coriander seed	1 oz.	lime juice

1 Place the salmon, skin side down, in a pan.

2 Combine all remaining ingredients in a food processor. Grind until the mixture is still fairly rough.

3 Spread the seasoning mixture evenly over each side of the salmon.

4 Marinate salmon in the refrigerator for at least 36 hours.

5 When ready to use, remove salmon from the marinade. Wash salmon under cold water to remove the seasoning residue. Drain on paper towels.

6 Cut salmon diagonally as thinly and as large as possible. Serve cold.

Ceviche of Bay Scallops

Serves 8

16 oz.	bay scallops, shelled
1 oz.	lime juice
$1\frac{1}{2}$	tomatoes, peeled, seeded, and chopped
1	avocado, chopped
$\frac{1}{2}$ oz.	cilantro (fresh coriander), finely chopped
1	fresh (hot) green chili, finely chopped
dash	salt
dash	black pepper, freshly ground

1 Mix all the ingredients together in a bowl.

2 Cover and marinate in the refrigerator for 24 hours.

3 Serve cold.

Gravlax has become the popular name for gravad lax (dill-cured salmon).

Fennel: An herb that is ground and used to flavor fish sauces and stews.

In this ceviche, the scallops are "cooked" by the action of the lime juice.

Seafood Salad

8 oz.	cleaned calamari
4 oz.	olive oil
1	garlic clove, crushed
5 oz.	onion, cut in julienne slices
3 oz.	dry white wine
	salt
	white pepper, freshly ground
dash	dried thyme leaves
dash	dried basil leaves
6 oz.	octopus
3	white peppercorns
1	bay leaf
8 oz.	conch, cooked
2	lemons, squeezed for the juice
3 oz.	celery, Chinese cut (diagonally)
¼ oz.	fresh flat-leaf parsley, chopped

1 Cut the calamari in medium-size rounds.

2 In a skillet, heat the olive oil. Add the garlic and sauté very briefly. Add the onion and sauté for about half a minute. Stir in the calamari, wine, salt, pepper, thyme, and basil; simmer (do not boil) for about 6 to 8 minutes. Place in a bowl.

3 While you are proceeding with step 2, at the same time, cook the octopus in water with the salt, peppercorns, and the bay leaf for about 35 minutes. The octopus will turn red.

4 When the octopus is tender, peel off the outer skin. Chill to slice easily. After octopus is chilled, cut in thin slices on a slicing machine or by hand.

5 Discard the intestines from the conch. Slice conch as thinly as possible.

6 Add the lemon juice to the calamari while still hot. Combine with the octopus and conch. Season again, if necessary.

7 When the seafood is cool, add the celery and parsley; correct the seasonings. Arrange on lettuce leaves. Serve cold.

When making salad dressing or mayonnaise, you need to use both hands—one to pour the oil, the other for the whisk. When using a stainless-steel mixing bowl, first wet a kitchen towel, folding it in a 4×4-inch square. Set the bowl on the top of the wet towel. The towel will keep the bowl more stationary as you mix.

Basil: A plant cultivated in Europe as an aromatic potherb. It is used to flavor sauces and stews.

Cilantro Dressing

2 oz.	lemon juice, freshly squeezed
¾ oz.	garlic, minced
pinch	cilantro (fresh coriander), chopped
9 oz.	olive oil
1 oz.	soy sauce
	salt
	white pepper, freshly ground
	cayenne pepper to taste

1 Combine the lemon juice, garlic, and coriander.

2 Slowly beat in the oil and soy sauce. Season to taste with salt and white and cayenne peppers. Serve cold.

1971

"This O.K. with knackwurst?"

Pike and Spinach Pâté

Serves 12–14

1 lb.	Boston sole, skinned, boned and filleted
2 lbs.	yellow pike, skinned, boned and filleted
	salt
	white pepper, freshly ground
dash	nutmeg, freshly grated
2	egg whites
24 oz.	heavy cream
½ lb.	fresh spinach leaves, cooked, drained, and coarsely chopped, then ground
4 oz.	unsalted butter for buttering pan and top of pâté
	Lemon Mayonnaise Sauce (recipe follows)

1 Grind the sole fillets; grind separately 1 pound of the pike fillets. Combine the ground sole and pike, and grind twice, as finely as possible. Cut the remaining pike fillets into ½-inch strips. Set aside the strips until ready to layer the pâté.

2 In a bowl, season the ground fillets with salt, pepper, and nutmeg. Beating on medium speed in a mixer, add the egg whites.

3 Gradually add the heavy cream while mixing constantly. Set aside half of the mixture. Add the ground spinach to the other half of the mixture.

4 Butter a 2½-quart mould. Spread two-thirds of the white mixture on the bottom of the mould. Continue layering as follows: Spread one-third of the spinach mixture about 1 inch thick over the white layer; top with half of the pike fillet strips; spread another one-third of the spinach mixture over the strips; add another layer of the remaining pike strips and a layer of the remaining spinach mixture. Top with the remaining one-third white mixture to seal the pâté. Butter the top and cover with foil.

5 Place the mould in a water bath, approximately halfway up the mould. Bake at 250°F for 1 to 1¼ hours. Remove from oven and cool at room temperature. Refrigerate until ready to use.

6 Unmould by loosening the sides with a sharp knife and either heating the bottom of the mould in a hot-water bath or over medium heat. Unmould directly on a plate or slicing board. Serve cold with Lemon Mayonnaise Sauce.

Lemon Mayonnaise Sauce

12 oz.	mayonnaise
1	lemon, squeezed for the juice
½ oz.	tomato paste
1½ oz.	cucumber, finely chopped
½ oz.	Pernod liqueur
4 oz.	unsweetened heavy cream, whipped
	salt and freshly ground white pepper

1 In a bowl, mix the mayonnaise and lemon juice with the tomato paste, cucumbers, and Pernod.

2 Fold the whipped cream into the sauce. Season with salt and pepper.

3 Chill the sauce. Serve with the pâté.

Appetizer Wines

The appetizer that begins each meal sets the style for the rest of the dinner. When you plan your menu, it is just as important to choose the appetizer and accompanying wine as you would the main course. After all, an appetizer is something that excites or whets the appetite. It gets you ready for the main event.

Whatever appetizer you choose to have at a restaurant, it will be smaller and lighter than the main course. Keep in mind that the idea behind any meal is a progression of wine and food. At the Cellar in the Sky, the meal begins with the lightest-style wine, followed by two medium-bodied wines, and finishes off with a full-bodied wine. Customarily, the first wine is white because they are generally—but not always—lighter in style than red wines. The cliché "white before red" usually holds true.

Sea Scallops with Two Caviars

Serves 8

32 oz.	sea scallops
6 oz.	unsalted butter
2 oz.	brandy
14 oz.	heavy cream (35% fat)
10 oz.	White Wine Sauce (page 100)
2 oz.	golden whitefish, lumpfish, or imported sturgeon caviar
2 oz.	pink salmon caviar
1	celery leaf
16	Puff Pastry (page 60), cut in fleurons

1 Slice the scallops in half horizontally. In a skillet, sauté the scallops briefly in the butter, but do not overcook.

2 Pour the brandy over the scallops and flambé. When the flame subsides, remove the scallops. Set aside and keep warm.

3 Add cream and reduce over low heat. Add White Wine Sauce.

4 Arrange the scallops nicely on a plate and top with the sauce. Alternate with a dab of red and black caviar on top of each scallop. Garnish with a celery leaf and puff pastry fleurons. Serve warm.

Sterling Sauvignon Blanc— Napa Valley, California
A light-style, dry white wine is most suitable to have with this dish, and the Sterling Sauvignon Blanc is an especially appropriate choice. In most cases, Sauvignon Blanc is lighter than Chardonnay. In my opinion, Sterling's Sauvignon Blanc is even lighter in style than others from California, plus it offers a crisp, dry acidity that complements both the scallops and the caviar. You can usually rely on Sterling's wines, since the winery opened in 1969 and has consistently been producing high-quality wines.

STERLING VINEYARDS.

ESTATE BOTTLED

1984

Sauvignon Blanc

NAPA VALLEY

GROWN, PRODUCED AND BOTTLED BY
STERLING VINEYARDS
CALISTOGA, NAPA VALLEY CA
ALC 12.5% BY VOL · BW CA 4533

To make fleurons, first roll out the Puff Pastry Dough (see recipe, page 60) until it is ⅛-inch thin. Using one side of the rounded edge of a 2½-inch cookie cutter, cut the dough into half moons and baste with egg wash. Bake in a preheated 375°F oven for 8 minutes. Use as a garnish for Poached Fish with White Wine Sauce, Lobster Sauce, and other dishes.

Scallops of Salmon in Chive Sauce

Serves 8

40 oz.	salmon fillet
	salt
½	lemon, squeezed for the juice
1 oz.	all-purpose flour
4 oz.	unsalted butter
2 oz.	dry white wine
5 oz.	White Fish Stock (page 154)
5 oz.	Crème Fraîche (page 36)
3	bunches chive, finely cut

1 Clean the salmon; slice diagonally ¼-inch thin into 8 salmon scallops. Season the scallops of salmon lightly with salt and lemon juice.

2 Sprinkle with the flour; sauté in hot melted butter, using a nonstick pan, for 1 minute on each side. Set fish aside on a warmed platter.

3 Deglaze with the wine.

4 Reduce the fish stock. Add the crème fraîche and simmer until the sauce coats a spoon.

5 Adjust the seasoning to taste. Add the chive and ladle onto a plate or platter.

6 Place scallops of salmon on top. Serve warm.

Hot Chicken Liver in Puff Pastry

Serves 8

8 oz.	boneless pork loin	¼ tsp.	dried marjoram
4 oz.	fatback		white pepper, freshly ground
5 oz.	chicken liver, cleaned and veined for grinding	5 oz.	Crème Fraîche (page 36)
1 oz.	unsalted butter	40 oz.	Puff Pastry (page 60)
3 oz.	chicken liver, diced	1	egg, lightly beaten
¾ oz.	shallot, finely chopped		Fresh Tomato Sauce (page 153)
⅛ oz.	fresh parsley, finely chopped		
	salt		

1 In a meat grinder, using the medium blade, grind together the pork, fatback, and the 5 oz. of chicken liver.

2 Melt the butter in a skillet and sauté the 3 oz. diced chicken liver and the shallot.

3 To make the stuffing, mix by hand all the remaining ingredients except the Puff Pastry and egg, including the seasonings and Crème Fraîche.

4 Roll out the puff pastry till ⅛-inch thick. Cut into 3-inch circles, using a 3-inch cookie cutter. Divide into 2 groups. Place mounds of stuffing in the middle of half of the pastry circles and cover each with another pastry circle. Press edges firmly to seal. Brush the tops with egg wash.

5 Bake at 350°F for 15 to 20 minutes until golden brown. Serve hot with Fresh Tomato Sauce.

Snails in Brie Butter

Serves 8

(6 pieces per person)

48	canned snails
6 oz.	unsalted butter
½ oz.	shallot, chopped
4 oz.	dry white wine
1 lb.	unsalted butter, at room temperature
8 oz.	ripe Brie, at room temperature
2 oz.	fresh basil, chopped
1 oz.	shallot, chopped
3 oz.	ground hazelnut (filbert) flour, available in specialty shops
1 oz.	Pernod liqueur
	salt, to taste
	white pepper, freshly ground

1 Rinse and drain the snails. In a skillet, heat the 6 oz. of butter and sauté the ½ oz. of shallot. Add the snails and sauté.

2 Deglaze with the wine; simmer until the liquid evaporates.

3 *To make the Brie butter:* Whip the 1 lb. of butter in a bowl. Remove the skin from the Brie and add the soft part of the Brie to the whipped butter. Beat until blended.

4 Add the basil, 1 oz. of shallot, hazelnut flour, Pernod, and salt.

5 Place snails in the dishes and top with the Brie butter and pepper.

6 Bake in a preheated oven at 375°F for about 12 minutes or until butter foams and becomes lightly brown. Serve immediately. Serve with warm, crusty French bread.

For this recipe, you will need 8 ovenproof snail dishes.

Hugel Riesling—Alsace, France
People are so accustomed to having snails in a garlic sauce that it's almost expected. Instead of using garlic, our chef adds a new dimension with the Brie cheese for this dish. Not only the taste but the texture is different because of the Brie. I find it appropriate to use a French white wine because the Brie is a French cheese. My choice is the Hugel Riesling because it's a well-known producer and the wine has enough acidity and body to cut through the creaminess of the Brie butter sauce. Look for the excellent 1985 vintage, which has more body than you will ordinarily find in an Alsatian Riesling.

Glen Ellen Sauvignon Blanc— Sonoma County, California

There are divided opinions when it comes to the use of cilantro (fresh coriander) and deciding which wine to serve with it. The problem is that it can be an overpowering flavor. The chef at Windows on the World uses cilantro with great care, making absolutely certain that it will dominate neither the food nor the wine. I would choose another light-bodied Sauvignon Blanc for this appetizer. Glen Ellen's Sauvignon Blanc has excellent varietal characteristics and has taken some top awards at major wine tastings. It is among the top-five Sauvignon Blancs of California.

Shrimp in Cilantro Sauce

Serves 8

40	large shrimps, 15 per pound, shelled and deveined
dash	salt
	white pepper, freshly ground
½	lemon, squeezed for the juice
dash	Worcestershire sauce
6 oz.	vegetable oil
4 oz.	unsalted butter
1½ oz.	shallot, finely chopped
4 oz.	dry white wine
10 oz.	White Fish Stock (page 154)
10 oz.	heavy cream
1 oz.	cilantro (fresh coriander), chopped
	whole cilantro leaves for garnish

1　In a flat bowl, season the shrimps with salt, pepper, lemon juice, and a dash of Worcestershire sauce.

2　In a skillet or sauté pan, heat the oil until very hot; add the shrimps and sauté on each side for about 1½ minutes. Remove from the skillet and set aside.

3　Pour fat out of the skillet and add the butter and shallot. Sauté for about 1 minute on low heat. Deglaze with white wine; reduce the sauce. Stir in the fish stock.

4　Add the heavy cream and simmer to the desired consistency. Strain the sauce.

5　Add the chopped cilantro and bring to a boil.

6　*To serve*: Arrange shrimps on a plate; ladle the sauce over the shrimps and garnish with cilantro leaves.

Beef Consommé

Serves 8 (Yields 2 quarts)

1½ lbs.	*lean beef from the neck and chuck*
3 oz.	*carrot*
4 oz.	*leek*
3 oz.	*celery*
3	*egg whites*
2 qts.	*White Beef Stock (page 74)*
½	*unpeeled onion*
10	*white peppercorns*
1	*bay leaf*
	salt

Helen C. Hokinson

"It seems to have gone downhill terribly—last summer they always put a teaspoonful of sherry in the consommé."

1 Grind the beef, carrot, leek, and celery through the coarse blade of a meat grinder.

2 Mix with the egg whites and a little cold water and let it rest for about 1 hour.

3 Put the mixture in a large pot; then add the completely fat-free beef stock and mix well.

4 Brown the half onion in a skillet or over an open flame (this is done so that the consommé will have a nice color). Add the onion to the pot.

5 Set the pot over low heat and slowly bring to the boiling point, stirring occasionally with a wooden spoon; be sure to mix the bottom of the pot carefully.

6 Lower the heat and skim off the fat and foam. Then add the peppercorns and bay leaf. Simmer gently for about 30 minutes.

7 Strain through cheesecloth; cool. Refrigerate until ready to use. Serve warm.

As a soup garnish for beef or chicken consommé, try the following ideas: blanched vegetables cut in julienne strips; fine, thinly sliced pancakes; semolina quenelles; fine pasta (vermicelli); sliced mushrooms and watercress leaves.

Drawing by Helen E. Hokinson;
© 1942, 1970
The New Yorker Magazine, Inc.

Chicken Consommé

Serves 8–10

2	chicken legs	2 qts.	White Chicken Stock (page 77)
2 oz.	leek	½ oz.	mushroom stems
2 oz.	celery	½ oz.	parsley stems
2 oz.	carrot	½	bay leaf
1	egg white	5	white peppercorns

1 Debone the chicken legs and trim off any fat.

2 Grind the chicken, leek, celery, carrot and mushroom stems through the coarse blade of a meat grinder.

3 Mix thoroughly with the egg white; add a few pieces of crushed ice. Let rest for 30 minutes.

4 Place mixture in a large pot. Pour in the chicken stock and mix well.

5 Bring to a boil over low heat, stirring on the bottom of the pot cautiously. Simmer for about 30 minutes. Strain the consommé through cheesecloth and degrease with a paper napkin.

Lobster Consommé

Serves 8–10

½ lb.	white fish fillets,	½ lb.	lobster bones,
	such as sole,		crushed
	flounder, or halibut,	2	egg whites
	and trimmings	1 qt.	Lobster Stock
2 oz.	celery		(page 39)
2 oz.	leek	½	bay leaf
1 oz.	shallot	5	white peppercorns
	½ oz. parsley stems		

1 Grind the fish fillets and bones with the celery, leek, and shallot through the coarse blade of a meat grinder. Mix with the crushed lobster bones.

2 Add the egg whites and some crushed ice; let rest for 30 minutes.

3 Place the mixture in a large pot and add the Lobster Stock with the spices and parsley stems.

4 Over low heat, bring to a boil; lower the heat and simmer for half an hour.

5 Strain through cheesecloth and correct the seasonings.

During my chef apprenticeship in Austria, we often strained sauces through heavy cheesecloth in a very practical way: Invert a small stool and place a deep bowl on the seat. Tie the cheesecloth from the top of the stool legs. Pour the sauce into the cheesecloth and let the sauce drain.

To remove the fat from stocks, soups, and consommés, use an unfolded paper napkin. Hold the napkin on either side with both hands and slice it over the surface of the liquid. It will absorb the fat. Repeat this procedure 2 or 3 times, discarding the napkin after each time.

Lobster Consommé has a very strong flavor. Therefore, plan to serve a half cupful or just a small taste.

When using a cheesecloth, always rinse the cloth thoroughly before each new use. There may still be some detergent in the fabric after it has been laundered.

Cream of Zucchini Soup

Serves 8

8 oz.	unsalted butter
3 oz.	onion, diced
1½ lbs.	zucchini, sliced
2 oz.	all-purpose flour (optional)
1 qt.	White Chicken Stock (page 77)
1 oz.	onion, diced
½ lb.	zucchini, diced ⅛-inch thick
14 oz.	heavy cream
4 oz.	canned whole tomatoes, drained and diced
1	sprig fresh oregano, chopped

1   In a soup pot, melt 6 oz. of the butter and sauté the 3 oz. of diced onion. Add the sliced zucchini and sauté. Add the flour (if you plan to serve the soup hot) and stir thoroughly.

2   Pour in the chicken stock and simmer for about 20 minutes. Purée in a blender until smooth.

3   Heat the remaining 2 oz. of butter in a soup pot; add the 1 oz. of diced onion and diced zucchini, and sauté. Stir in the heavy cream and the puréed zucchini soup. Simmer for 5 minutes.

4   Add the diced tomatoes and the fresh oregano; correct seasonings. Serve hot or cold.

In this creamy soup, some of the zucchini will be puréed and some diced. You may serve this soup hot or cold, but if it's cold, omit the flour.

Cream of Asparagus Soup with Mint

Serves 8

1 lb.	tiny green asparagus
6 oz.	unsalted butter
3 oz.	onion, diced
3 oz.	all-purpose flour
1 qt.	White Chicken Stock (page 77)
16 oz.	heavy cream
	salt to taste
	white pepper, freshly ground
dash	ground nutmeg
¼	lemon, squeezed for the juice
1	fresh mint sprig

Mint: The name of several aromatic herbaceous plants, popular for their tonic properties.

(continued)

1 Wash the asparagus, and cut into 1-inch pieces; keep the tips separated from the other pieces.

2 Melt the butter in a soup pot; add the onion and cook until transparent. Add the asparagus pieces (not the tips) and dash with flour; stir thoroughly.

3 Pour in the chicken stock and bring to a boil, stirring well with a whisk. Simmer for about 30 minutes over low heat.

4 Place in a blender and purée until smooth. Then strain through a Chinese strainer into the soup pot.

5 Bring to a boil and add the reserved asparagus tips; simmer for about 2 minutes. Add the heavy cream and season the soup with salt, pepper, ground nutmeg, and lemon juice.

6 Sprinkle with mint leaves when ready to serve. Serve hot.

Conch Chowder

Serves 8

8 oz.	fresh conch, medium
4 oz.	unsalted butter
3	onions, diced
1 oz.	green bell pepper, diced
4 oz.	large potato, peeled and finely diced
1 qt.	White Fish Stock (page 154)
16 oz.	canned clam juice
	salt to taste
dash	cayenne pepper
	black pepper, freshly ground
dash	Tabasco sauce
4 oz.	dry white wine
6 oz.	okra, finely sliced
6 oz.	tomato, peeled and diced
$1/16$ oz.	fresh flat-leaf parsley, chopped

1 Cut conch into fine julienne strips.

2 Heat the butter in a skillet. Add the conch, diced onions, pepper, and potato, and sauté, stirring occasionally.

3 Add the fish stock, clam juice, and the seasonings; simmer for about 20 minutes.

4 During the last 5 minutes of cooking, add the wine, okra, and tomatoes.

5 Garnish with chopped parsley and serve hot.

Strainers: Chinese strainer (Chinoise); bouillon strainer; mesh strainer.

Cayenne: A variety of pepper. The powdered pod and seeds of various species of capsicums. Cayenne has a savory, hot flavor.

Simmer: A slow, gentle boil (200°F).

Cellar in the Sky Menu with International Wines and Cheeses

Semi-hard Cheeses

Soft-ripened Cheeses

R

Blue-veined Cheeses

Chèvres (Goat Cheeses)

Windows' Chocolate Sabayon Cake (*top left*) Krokant Cake (*top right*)
Chocolate Truffles (*middle*) Apple Pancake Tart (*bottom*)

Dark Chocolate Mousse Terrine (*left*) Mocha Mousse Terrine (*right*)
White Chocolate Mousse Terrine (*middle*)

Petits Fours

Tropical Fruit Soup

Dried Fruits in Filo
with Apricot Sorbet

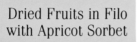

Amaretto Cheesecake   Gâteau de Pithiviers

Viennese Apple Strudel   White Chocolate Mousse

Weinbeisser
and
Sugared Fried Walnuts

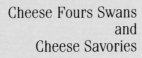

Cheese Fours Swans
and
Cheese Savories

W

(left to right)

Cellar Manager
Steven Rosenbloom

Cellarmaster
Barry Mills

Wine Stewards
Alec Brough
and
Riccardo Legnaro

(left to right)

Pastry Chefs
Peter Begusch
and
Michelle Tampakis

Sous Chefs
Leopold Bauernberger
Siegfried Hohaus
and
Karl Schmid

X

Corn and Crab Chowder

Serves 8

12 oz.	frozen corn kernels
4 oz.	unsalted butter
2 oz.	onion, diced
1 oz.	leek, diced
1	garlic clove, crushed
12 oz.	White Fish Stock (page 154)
20 oz.	White Chicken Stock (page 77)
2 oz.	unsalted butter
4 oz.	shiitake mushrooms, sliced
8 oz.	heavy cream
	salt to taste
	white pepper, freshly ground
	Tabasco sauce
1	bunch scallions, green parts only
8 oz.	lump crab meat

1 In salted water, separately cook 3 oz. of the corn kennels and set aside.

2 Heat the 4 oz. of butter in a cooking pot; add the onion and cook until transparent. Add the leek, garlic, and uncooked 9 oz. of corn kernels. Stir and add the fish and chicken stocks. Bring to a boil and simmer till the corn is tender.

3 Place in a blender and purée until smooth. Heat the 2 oz. butter and sauté the mushrooms for 1 minute. Stir in the heavy cream and the puréed stock; simmer gently for 5 minutes.

4 Add the cooked corn kernels and the crab meat.

5 Season with salt, pepper, and Tabasco sauce.

6 Thinly slice the green parts of the scallion and sprinkle on the soup just before serving. Serve hot.

Leek: A well-known vegetable with a bulbous root. The national badge of the Welsh.

Sauté (pan-fry): Using a skillet or pan, to lightly fry in oil.

Tomato Bisque

Serves 8

16 oz.	canned whole peeled tomatoes	1 qt.	White Chicken Stock (page 77)
2 oz.	unsalted butter	8 oz.	heavy cream
3 oz.	onion, diced		salt to taste
2	garlic cloves, crushed	¼ oz.	sugar
			white pepper, freshly ground
2 oz.	tomato purée		
2	fresh thyme sprigs		

Thyme: A genus of small shrubs. A favorite because of its aromatic odor.

(continued)

1   Squeeze the tomatoes and strain, saving the juice. Finely chop the tomatoes and reserve 2 oz. for the garnish.

2   Heat the butter in a soup pot and sauté the onions until transparent. Add the crushed garlic and sauté for a few seconds; then add the tomato purée and sauté. Add the chopped tomatoes, tomato juice, and chicken stock; stir and bring to a boil.

3   Simmer for about 20 minutes; blend at low speed until fine and smooth but do not strain.

4   Pour back into the pot and add the heavy cream. Season with the salt, pepper, and sugar.

5   Simmer for a few minutes. Before serving, sprinkle with fresh thyme leaves, whole or chopped, and the reserved chopped tomatoes. Serve hot or cold with toasted garlic bread.

Black Bean Soup with Chorizo

Serves 8

8 oz.	black beans, soaked in water overnight	48 oz.	White Veal Stock (page 31)
3 oz.	vegetable oil	16 oz.	bacon or ham bone pieces or end cuts
1 oz.	onion, diced		
1 oz.	carrot, diced	1	fresh thyme sprig
1 oz.	celery, diced		salt to taste
1 oz.	leek, diced		white pepper, freshly ground
2	garlic cloves, chopped		
8 oz.	chorizo, cooked		

1   Wash the beans in cold water. Cover with water again and soak overnight; drain.

2   In a soup pot, heat the oil and sauté the onion, carrot, celery, and leek. Add the garlic and the beans. Pour in the stock. Bring to a boil and add the bacon or ham pieces.

3   Simmer until the beans are tender. Remove the ham or bacon. With a slotted spoon, lift about 3 oz. of the cooked beans for garnish.

4   Purée the rest of the beans with the soup in a blender. Strain through a fine Chinese strainer directly into a casserole.

5   Bring the soup to a boil. Add the thyme leaves and the reserved whole beans. Season with salt and pepper.

6   Slice the chorizo and add to the soup. Serve hot.

Main Course Wines

Many people consider the wine that is served with the main course to be the most important of the meal. For dinners with which you are serving more than one wine or several courses, you need a medium- to full-bodied wine to go along with the main course. When you "graze," you may sample several light dishes or appetizers, until you've had enough to call it a meal. There is nothing wrong in drinking a lighter-style wine in this case, and it may even be your preference.

Another school of thought contends that the most full-bodied and best wine should be saved for the cheese course at the end of the meal. This is the philosophy at the Cellar in the Sky, which means that we usually try to match the medium-bodied wines to the main courses.

Sautéed Soft-shell Crabs with Cucumbers

Serves 8

24	soft-shell crabs, (hotel prime size)	6 oz.	unsalted butter
1½ lbs.	cucumber		white pepper, freshly ground
	salt	½	lemon, squeezed for the juice
6 oz.	vegetable oil		
4 oz.	all-purpose flour	¼ bunch	fresh dill

1 Have the crabs cleaned by your fishmonger.

2 Peel the cucumber and remove the pulp. Cut the cucumber diagonally into ½-inch slices. Salt the slices and set aside for 1 hour; then wash off and dry.

3 Heat the oil in a large skillet. Salt the crabs and dust with flour. Sauté quickly on both sides until crisp. Remove from the skillet and set aside.

4 Drain the oil and replace with the butter. Heat the butter and add the cucumber slices; sauté for 1 to 2 minutes. Season with salt, pepper, lemon juice and pinched leaves of dill.

5 Arrange the crab on plates or a platter. Ladle cucumber and butter sauce from the skillet over it. Serve warm with boiled new potatoes.

RUTHERFORD HILL

1983
Napa Valley
CHARDONNAY
Jaeger Vineyards

PRODUCED AND BOTTLED BY RUTHERFORD HILL WINERY
RUTHERFORD, CALIF. USA · ALCOHOL 13.8% BY VOLUME

Rutherford Hill Chardonnay— Napa Valley, California
Sautéed Soft-Shell Crabs is an extremely simple recipe to prepare. That's why I like the medium-bodied Rutherford Hill Chardonnay. It is one of the most reliable, medium-bodied Chardonnays in California. If you can't get a Rutherford Hill Chardonnay, look carefully at other Chardonnays for one with similar varietal characteristics.

Dill: An aromatic herb grown for its seed. Used in pickles and sauces. Fresh dill leaves are used in many dishes.

Shrimp in Leek with Tomatoes and Broccoli

Serves 6

30	large shrimps, peeled and deveined
	salt
	white pepper, freshly ground
5	leeks, washed, cut in half lengthwise, and blanched
1 oz.	shallot, chopped
4 oz.	olive oil
1	garlic clove, chopped
8 oz.	Tomato Concassé (recipe follows)
4 oz.	dry white wine
1 oz.	Cognac
16 oz.	White Wine Sauce (recipe follows)
8 oz.	fresh broccoli florets, cooked

1   Season the shrimps with salt and pepper. Partially wrap each shrimp in a blanched leek strip.

2   Sauté the shallot in 1 oz. of the oil and add the garlic. Then stir in all the Tomato Concassé and wine. Season with salt and pepper. Simmer for approximately 10 minutes and set aside.

3   In another saucepan, sauté the wrapped shrimps in 3 oz. of oil until just pink. Deglaze with the Cognac.

4   Pour a little White Wine Sauce on a plate. Arrange the shrimps on the sauce and spoon a little of the cooked Tomato Concassé in the middle. Surround the shrimps with the broccoli florets.

Tomato Concassé

4 tomatoes

1   Core the tomatoes and dip into boiling water for about 10 seconds.

2   Quickly cool the tomatoes in cold water and peel off the skins.

3   Cut tomatoes in half and squeeze out the seeds. Dice into ⅛-inch pieces.

WHITE WINE SAUCE   **Yields 16 oz.**

3 oz.	unsalted butter	4 oz.	dry white wine
½ oz.	shallot, chopped and peeled	6 oz.	heavy cream
3 oz.	all-purpose flour		salt
16 oz.	White Fish Stock (page 154)		white pepper, freshly ground

1   In a casserole, heat the butter. Add the shallot and sauté for a few seconds; then add the flour. Sauté for half a minute.

2   Add the fish stock and wine, stirring with a whisk; bring to a boil and simmer for 20 minutes.

3   Strain through cheesecloth or a Chinese strainer into a saucepan. Bring to a boil. Stir in the heavy cream and salt and pepper.

Roast Squab
with Lentils

Serves 8

12 oz.	lentils
6 oz.	smoked bacon, diced
3 oz.	onion, diced
2 oz.	red bell pepper, diced
1 qt.	White Beef Stock (page 74)
	bouquet garni: 1 sprig fresh parsley, 1 sprig fresh thyme, and 1 bay leaf
8	squabs (16 oz. each)
6 oz.	vegetable oil
2 tbsp.	salt
½ tbsp.	black pepper, freshly ground
½ tsp.	fresh lemon thyme, chopped
½ tsp.	fresh rosemary, chopped
16 oz.	squab jus (made in step 3)
6 oz.	unsalted butter
30	fresh chervil leaves

1 Soak the lentils overnight in lightly salted water. Next day, rinse in running water and drain.

2 In a casserole, sauté the bacon until crisp. Stir in the onion and cook for about 2 minutes. Add the red bell pepper and cook for about 2 minutes. Add the drained lentils and enough of the beef stock to cover the lentils. Stir the bouquet garni into the food. Cook till lentils are *al dente*. Set aside and keep warm.

3 Trim the squabs. Make squab *jus*: In a saucepan, boil the giblet and wings in 3 cups of water for 30 minutes. Strain the *jus* and measure 10 oz.

4 Season the squabs with salt, black pepper, half of the thyme, and rosemary.

5 In a heated roasting pan, sear both sides of the squab breasts in the vegetable oil. Roast at 350°F for about 7 to 10 minutes or until the squabs are still rare; let rest for 10 minutes.

6 Remove squabs from pan. Pour off the fat and deglaze the pan with the *jus*.

7 Reheat the lentils in the casserole, add remaining chopped herbs.

8 Whisk the butter into the squab *jus*.

9 Split the squabs. Arrange on plates on top of the lentils. Sprinkle with chervil leaves and pour *jus* on each side of the lentils.

Bay Leaf: The aromatic leaf of the laurel tree. The whole dried leaf is used to increase the flavor of many foods.

Antinori, Chianti Classico
The Antinori Chianti Classico is a good choice with Roast Squab with Lentils because the medium-bodied red wine complements the texture of the meat. Chianti is one of the most underrated red wines in the world, and it represents a great value. There are levels of Chianti to look for: Chianti, Chianti Classico, and Chianti Classico Riserva. For this dish, I suggest either a Chianti Classico or the Chianti Classico Riserva, which are more richly flavored than ordinary Chianti. Another reliable name in the wine industry, Antinori has been producing wines since 1385, and to this day they continue to experiment with new and improved wines.

Chervil: A hairy herb of the carrot family. Chervil has longish, grooved fruits, common in the fields of Great Britain.

Sliced Veal in Cream Sauce with Mushrooms and Avocado

Serves 8

32 oz.	leg of veal, thinly sliced
	salt
	white pepper, freshly ground
3 oz.	unsalted butter
½ oz.	shallot, chopped
5 oz.	fresh mushrooms or shiitake mushrooms
2 oz.	dry white wine
6 oz.	heavy cream
1	small avocado, diced
	fresh chive, finely cut

1   Season the sliced veal with salt and pepper.

2   In a skillet, heat three-fourths of the butter until the butter is very hot but not brown. Sauté the veal in the butter for about 1½ minutes, but leave it pink.

3   Remove the veal with a slotted spoon. Add the remaining butter and the shallot. Sauté for about half a minute. Stir in the mushrooms and sauté for about 1 minute.

4   Deglaze with the wine and reduce to about half. Add the cream and reduce till the sauce coats a spoon. Taste and correct the seasonings.

5   Add the veal slices, but do not cook (meat will become tough).

6   Add the diced avocados. Serve on a dinner plate with buttered fettucine or pilaf. Garnish with the chive.

Sautéed Chicken with Walnuts and Broccoli

Serves 2 to 3

1	broccoli stalk	½ oz.	shallot, finely chopped
2	double chicken breasts	1 oz.	brandy
	salt	4 oz.	walnut halves
	pepper	12 oz.	heavy cream
1 oz.	butter	1 oz.	unsalted butter

Puligny-Montrachet (Ropiteau Frères)—Burgundy, France

Veal goes well with either a full-bodied white wine or a light red wine. For this particular dish, I prefer a white wine, because the cream sauce is made with a white wine. I have chosen the Puligny-Montrachet to go with this dish because it is full flavored enough to cut through the creaminess of the sauce. Made from 100 percent Chardonnay grapes, the Puligny-Montrachet is an elegant, flavorful wine.

Deglaze: To add water, stock, wine, or other alcohol to roasting meat, bones or sautéing food in order to either finish the product or to loosen the roasting residue from the pan.

Gavi, Pio Cesare—Piedmont, Italy

Italian wines are famous for their reds. However, in the past few years, Italian winemakers have put a great deal of effort into their white wines. In fact, they produce some very good Chardonnays, among others. These new Italian white wines are fuller and more flavorful than Soave, Verdicchio, and Pinot Grigio. For this chicken appetizer in a cream sauce, I chose a white Pio Cesare Gavi because the wine has enough body to stand up to the walnuts. In fact, this Gavi has a little more body than most others because Pio Cesare ages his wines in small oak barrels.

1   Trim the broccoli close to the florets; use only the florets for this dish. Steam florets for 1 minute and refresh in cold water; set aside.

2   Wash and pat the chicken dry. Cut into large chunks. Season chicken with salt and pepper.

3   In an 8-to-10-inch skillet, melt the butter over medium to high heat. Add the shallot and chicken and sauté quickly, browning the chicken. Add the brandy, let it warm for a moment and then flambé

4   When the flame subsides, remove the chicken to a serving dish. Arrange the broccoli around the chicken. Place the walnuts in the skillet and cook for 1 minute.

5   Pour in the cream and cook at a quick boil until the sauce is reduced to half. Remove the pan from the heat and stir in the remaining butter.

6   Pour sauce over the top. Serve immediately.

Beef Paillard with Fresh Horseradish

Serves 8

8	*boneless sirloin steaks (5 oz. each)*
	salt
	white pepper, freshly ground
6 oz.	*vegetable oil*
16 oz.	*Bordelaise Sauce (page 156)*
14 oz.	*fresh horseradish, medium-finely grated*
8	*egg yolks*
½ bunch	*fresh dill*

1   Thoroughly trim the steaks. *To make the paillards,* pound to ⅛-inch thickness or cut, butterfly style, and pound lightly.

2   Heat the oil in a large skillet; sauté the paillards rapidly on each side (do not cook them well done); set aside.

3   Pour off the fat and deglaze skillet with the Bordelaise Sauce. Strain the sauce.

4   Ladle the sauce on each plate. Place a paillard on the sauce. Make a nest of horseradish on the meat; then place the raw egg yolk (without the shell) in the nest. Garnish with a sprig of dill. Serve warm.

"Petit Club du Huit"
If you look ahead to my wine recommendation for Beef Medallions, you'll notice that I take the opposite stand here. I'm going to suggest that you have a lighter-style red wine with the Beef Paillard with Fresh Horseradish. First look at how the paillard is prepared. The beef is pounded for this recipe and has a much different texture than the Beef Medallions. Also, this recipe calls for horseradish and egg—not exactly what I'd like to wash down with Château Margaux. With these considerations in mind, I would look for a "Petit Château" wine. These are Bordeaux wines that are excellent in quality, but they are not classified growths like Château Lafite. I would suggest any of the following, which I refer to as the "Petit Club du Huit": Château Gloria, Château Angludet, Château Phélan-Ségur, Château Fourcas-Hosten, Château La Rose-Trintaudon, Château Greysac, Château Simard, and Château Monbousquet.

Serve this Beef Paillard with sautéed or steamed potatoes, and vegetables.

This Fricassee of Sea Scallops and Shrimps should be served with pilaf, buttered fettuccine or linguini, or another pasta.

Fricassee of Sea Scallops and Shrimps with Two Squashes

Serves 8

32 oz.	shelled sea scallops
16	shrimps, (25 to 30 per pound)
1	medium zucchini
1	medium yellow squash
6 oz.	unsalted butter
	salt
	white pepper, freshly ground
4 oz.	dry white wine
16 oz.	White Wine Sauce (page 100)
6 oz.	heavy cream
$\frac{1}{16}$ oz.	pink peppercorn
$\frac{1}{2}$ oz.	chive, cut
8	Puff Pastry (page 60), cut in fleurons

1 Clean the sea scallops, removing the muscles; slice each scallop against the grain into 2 to 3 pieces.

2 Shell and devein the shrimps; cut lengthwise in half.

3 Wash the zucchini and yellow squash. Scrape with an olive scoop or small Parisienne scoop on the side of the vegetables so that each piece has some skin left on. (If you do not have the above tools, cut the vegetables with a knife into ⅙-inch slices; then dice the vegetables.)

4 Heat half of the butter in a casserole. Season the sea scallops with salt and pepper and sauté in the butter for about 1 minute. Remove from the casserole and set aside on a plate.

5 Heat the remaining butter in the casserole. Add the seasoned shrimps, sautéing for 1 minute; remove from casserole and set aside.

6 Deglaze casserole with the wine and juice of the scallops and shrimps (including juices from the plate). Add the wine sauce and reduce; simmer for about 5 minutes. Then add the heavy cream. Cook slowly till the sauce coats a spoon. Strain the sauce through a fine Chinese strainer.

7 Blanch the scooped vegetables in salted water. Refresh with cold water; set aside to drain.

8 In a saucepan, mix scallops, shrimp, zucchini, and squash with the sauce. Heat and bring to a boil for a few seconds; correct seasoning.

9 *To serve*: Ladle in soup plates. Sprinkle with pink peppercorn and cut chive. Garnish with the puff pastry fleurons.

Chablis Premier Cru—Chablis, France, Albert Pic & Fils
There are many flavors in Fricassee of Sea Scallops and Shrimps with Two Squashes in cream sauce. It calls for a medium-bodied wine with enough flavor not to be overpowered by all of the taste sensations. That's why I recommend Chablis Premier Cru, made from 100 percent Chardonnay grapes. Chablis has good fruit and a nice acid balance that gets through the cream sauce. With a good 1985 vintage and a respected producer such as Albert Pic & Fils, you cannot go wrong.

Beef Medallions with Braised Shallots in Bordelaise Sauce with Zucchini and Tomatoes

Serves 8

12 oz.	small shallot, whole and peeled
8 oz.	unsalted butter
6 oz.	Bordeaux red wine
16 oz.	Bordelaise Sauce (page 156)
16	beef tenderloin medallions (3 oz. each)
	salt
	white pepper, freshly ground
6 oz.	olive oil
14 oz.	medium zucchini
4	whole ripe tomatoes 2½ inches in diameter
	fresh thyme leaves
2 oz.	parsley, chopped

1 In a saucepan, sauté the shallots in the butter until light golden. Add the wine and simmer gently for about 10 minutes. When the wine has nearly evaporated, add the Bordelaise Sauce. Bring to a boil and simmer to the desired consistency; set aside.

2 Season the medallions with salt and pepper. Heat the oil in a skillet and sauté the medallions to desired degree: rare, medium, or well done.

3 Thinly slice the unpeeled zucchini and tomatoes and place alternately on an oiled baking sheet. Season with salt and pepper. Bake at 375°F for about 6 to 8 minutes. Sprinkle with the thyme and keep warm.

4 Place a portion of the baked zucchini and tomatoes, and 2 beef medallions on each warmed dinner plate. Then cover the meat with braised shallot and sauce. Sprinkle with the chopped parsley. Serve warm.

The Big Eight
There comes a time in one's life to splurge. Although I'm very concerned about how much you spend on wine, once a year you should get carried away and buy that special wine. So now that you know what you're in for and you've already started saving your loose change, choose any one of the following to go with this hearty entrée of Beef Medallions with Braised Shallots in Bordelaise Sauce with Zucchini and Tomatoes: Château Lafite-Rothschild, Château Latour, Château Mouton-Rothschild, Château Haut-Brion, Château Margaux, Château Pétrus, Château Ausone, and Château Cheval Blanc. The vintages to look for are: '61, '66, '70, '78, and '79. (P.S. Keeping in mind how much these wines cost, I wouldn't want to use 6 ounces in the sauce!)

MIS EN BOUTEILLE AU CHÂTEAU

CHATEAU LAFITE-ROTHSCHILD

PRODUCE OF FRANCE PAUILLAC APPELLATION PAUILLAC CONTROLEE 75cl

DEPOSE SOCIÉTÉ CIVILE DU CHATEAU LAFITE ROTHSCHILD, PROPRIÉTAIRE A PAUILLAC (GIRONDE)

Vegetables

"*What kind of wine goes with no meat?*"

French-Fried Zucchini

Serves 8

1½ lbs.	zucchini, washed, unpeeled, with ends trimmed
4	eggs
	salt
	white pepper, freshly ground
10 oz.	all-purpose flour
20 oz.	bread crumbs
32 oz.	vegetable oil for frying
	coarse salt for sprinkling

1 Cut zucchini into strips about the size of ⅜-inch-thick french fries.

2 In a bowl, beat the eggs and season with salt and pepper.

3 A handful at a time, dip zucchini first into the flour, shaking off the excess, then into the eggs, and finally into the bread crumbs. Gently pat the zucchini strips to help the bread crumbs adhere. Place the coated zucchini strips on paper towels.

4 In a deep fryer, heat the oil to 325°F. Fry zucchini in small batches, just as many as will make a single layer in the fryer. Fry until golden brown. Remove with a skimmer and drain on paper towels.

5 Sprinkle with the coarse salt. Drain on a paper towel or napkin. Serve hot.

Excellent to serve with roast meat or fish.

Squash and zucchini are best when sautéed in butter or oil and seasoned with herbs. But squash and zucchini can be very different in taste when sliced thinly and marinated in oil, salt, pepper, and Worcestershire sauce, and then grilled over charcoal for your cookout or barbecue.

Drawing by Weber; © 1973
The New Yorker Magazine, Inc.

Pilaf with Pine Nuts

Serves 8

4 oz.	unsalted butter	1	bay leaf	
1 oz.	onion, finely chopped		salt	
12 oz.	long-grain rice	2 oz.	pine nuts	
24 oz.	White Chicken	¼ oz.	flat-leaf parsley,	
	Stock (page 77)		chopped	

1 Heat butter in a casserole; add the onion and sauté; then add the rice. Stir well and pour in the chicken stock. Bring to a boil and add the bay leaf and some salt, if needed.

2 Cover and cook in a preheated oven at 350°F for about 20 minutes.

3 Meanwhile, spread the pine nuts on a baking sheet. Toast pine nuts in the oven at 350°F until lightly golden.

4 Remove rice from the oven. Before stirring, remove the bay leaf; then add the pine nuts and parsley and stir well.

Serve this pilaf with chicken fricassee, veal dishes, or seafoods with sauce.

Turnip Purée with Diced Carrot

Serves 8

1 lb.	medium white	½ lb.	carrots, peeled
	turnips, peeled		white pepper,
½ lb.	Idaho potatoes,		freshly ground
	peeled	2 oz.	unsalted butter
	salt to taste		

1 Cut the turnips and potatoes in 1-inch cubes. Dice the carrots in ¼-inch dice.

2 In a large pot, over low heat, boil the turnips and potatoes in water with a pinch of salt for about 18 to 20 minutes or until tender. Remove from heat and drain.

3 Separately, boil the carrots in water with a pinch of salt for about 15 minutes or until tender; drain.

4 Mash the turnips and potatoes into a purée. Add the butter and taste to correct the seasoning.

5 Heat well, add the cooked carrots, mix again. Serve immediately.

Delicious with roast beef, lamb, or chicken.

Carrots can be peeled, cut, or diced. Or you can grate them. Save the green end of the carrots. Finely chop the greens. Then mix with the glazed carrots after cooking them. Add a pat of butter, a pinch of salt, and some sugar; cover and cook slowly. When the carrots become tender, reduce the liquid until only the butter glazes the carrots.

Baked Eggplant with Soy Sauce and Ginger

Serves 8

2 lbs.	small eggplant		1 oz.	sugar
¼ oz.	fresh ginger		2 oz.	vegetable oil
4 oz.	sweet soy sauce			salt to taste
8 oz.	rice wine			white pepper,
	(or dry white wine)			freshly ground

1   Peel the eggplant and cut in 1½-inch-high pieces. Place in salted water for about half an hour; then drain.

2   Grate or thinly slice the ginger; mix with soy sauce, wine, and sugar.

3   Place the eggplant upright in a flat, ovenproof dish. Pour soy sauce mixture over the eggplant.

4   Place on the top shelf of a preheated oven and bake at 400°F for 10 minutes. Turn the eggplant over (to color on each side). Return eggplant to the oven for another 10 minutes or until the eggplant is tender.

5   If the liquid evaporates too much, add a little warm water. Serve warm, with broiled fish or meat.

Steamed New Potatoes with Bacon and Thyme

Serves 8

24	small, white-skin new potatoes	6	bacon slices
		2	fresh thyme sprigs
	coarse salt		

1   Wash potatoes; cut off the tops and bottoms so that they stand up.

2   Scoop out the tops of potatoes with a Parisienne scoop spoon, leaving the potato sides with the skin on as side walls.

3   Slice the bacon in ⅛-inch strips and fill into the hole of the potato. Top with a sprig of fresh thyme and sprinkle with the salt.

4   Place, standing up, in an ovenproof dish. Pour a little water into the dish. Completely cover dish with aluminum foil, covering tightly on all sides.

5   Bake at 375°F for about 35 minutes. Remove aluminum foil before serving. Serve warm.

Do not use baking soda when boiling vegetables. It may bring out a nice color, but the vegetables become mushy very quickly.

Always salt the water before boiling the vegetables; and never cover the pan while boiling green vegetables. They will not stay green, and may turn gray.

108

Sautéed New Potatoes with Herbs

Serves 8

2½ lbs.	medium white-skin new potatoes	⅒ oz.	fresh parsley, chopped
6 oz.	vegetable oil	⅒ oz.	fresh thyme, chopped
4 oz.	unsalted butter white pepper, freshly ground	1	garlic clove, chopped
	salt		

1   Wash the potatoes, and cut in 6 to 8 wedges.

2   Place in a pot of salted water and bring to a boil. Drain and refresh potatoes with cold water; drain thoroughly.

3   In a roasting pan, heat the oil. Add the potatoes, browning on all sides. Then bake in oven at 375°F for about 10 minutes.

4   Drain off the oil and add the butter, stirring thoroughly with a spatula. Season with salt and pepper.

5   Add the herbs and mix. Serve warm.

Serve with meat roasts, or grilled or broiled fish.

String Beans Sautéed with Shallots

Serves 8

1½ lb.	string beans, cleaned salt		white pepper from the mill
4 oz.	unsalted butter	¼ oz.	fresh herbs (parsley, thyme, or others), chopped
1 oz.	shallot, finely chopped		
½	garlic clove, chopped		

1   Clean the string beans; break off both ends and pull the strings off.

2   Cook in salted water until al dente (still firm). Refresh them in cold running water.

3   In a skillet, heat the butter. Add the shallot and garlic; then add the string beans. Season with salt and pepper.

4   Sauté for about 2 minutes over medium heat. Add the fresh herbs before serving. Serve warm.

To prepare green vegetables, such as peas, string beans, and/or brussels sprouts: Just clean the vegetables and place them in salted boiling water and cook until al dente. Then strain and refresh with cold water. Set aside in a glass or china dish. Cover and refrigerate until needed. Vegetables keep for 1 to 2 days. To cook, sauté in fresh unsalted butter and season to your taste. Sprinkle with fresh herbs before serving.

String Beans Sautéed with Shallots make a fine accompaniment with grilled or sautéed fish or meat, such as beef, chicken, or lamb.

Dessert Wines

I have a confession to make: I'm not very enthusiastic about matching desserts with a sweet wine. For me, sweetness on top of sweetness simply does not work well. If I had my choice, I would enjoy the following dessert wines by themselves (at most, I would recommend serving cheese or fruit with them):

○ Auslese, Beerenauslese, Trockenbeerenauslese (Germany)
○ Sauternes, Barsac (Bordeaux, France)
○ Late Harvest Rieslings (California)
○ Port wine (Portugal)

As we've already mentioned, at the Cellar in the Sky, a dessert wine is part of the meal, but we serve it ten to fifteen minutes before the actual dessert to prepare you for what's to come. Also, the desserts that our chef creates are just as special as the wines. We don't try to specifically coordinate the last wine with the dessert because it would unnecessarily restrict the chef.

Here are some accepted wine and food combinations for dessert, plus some exceptions to the rule:

○ Serve medium- to full-bodied sweet dessert wine with foie gras or with certain cheeses such as Roquefort
○ Port with Stilton cheese
○ A light-style Sauternes as an apéritif

Gâteau de Pithiviers

Serves 10

12 oz.	Puff Pastry (page 60)
5 oz.	almond paste (available in specialty shops)
5 oz.	sugar
5 oz.	unsalted butter
4	eggs
4 oz.	all-purpose flour
2 oz.	apricot jam
5	apricots
1	egg for egg wash

1 *To prepare the pastry*: Roll out the puff dough till ⅛-inch thick.

2 Cut one 10-inch circle and one 12-inch circle.

3 *For the filling*: Combine the almond paste, sugar, and butter in a bowl. Beat with an electric mixer until fluffy.

4 Add the eggs, one at a time, and the flour. Remove from the mixer.

5 *To fill*: Place the 10-inch puff pastry circle on a baking sheet lined with parchment. Spread the apricot jam over the middle to within 2 inches of the edges; leave a 2-inch margin all around.

6 Cut the apricots in half and remove the pits. Arrange the halves on top of the jam. Mound the filling on the apricots, careful to preserve the margin all around.

7 Beat the whole egg lightly with a fork to make the egg wash. Brush some along the margin.

8 Place the 12-inch circle on top of the mounded filling. Press very firmly along edges to secure. Brush remaining egg wash on top of the dough.

9 Bake in a preheated 300°F oven for 1 hour or until firm and a small knife inserted in the middle comes out clean. Cool slightly before serving. Serve warm or cold. (Color photo on page V.)

When sugar is called for in the recipes, use granulated sugar. If the recipe requires powdered (confectioners') sugar, the ingredient list includes the word "powdered."

Dark Chocolate Mousse Terrine

Serves 20 (one loaf pan, 12 × 4 inches)

for MOUSSE

9 oz.	semisweet chocolate	6	egg whites
1 oz.	unsalted butter	3 oz.	heavy cream
4	egg yolks	¾ oz.	unflavored gelatin

for CHOCOLATE SPONGECAKE

3	eggs	¾ oz.	cocoa
2¼ oz.	sugar	1 oz.	raspberry
2 oz.	all-purpose flour		liqueur

for DECORATION

6 oz.   semisweet chocolate, melted

1 *For the mousse*: Chop the semisweet chocolate and melt in a bowl on top of a double boiler over hot, not boiling, water; add the butter.

2 Whip the egg yolks until foamy in another bowl.

3 Separately, whip the egg whites until soft peaks form.

4 Whip the heavy cream in another bowl until soft peaks form.

5 Whisk the egg yolk into the melted chocolate-butter mixture.

6 Fold in the egg whites, using a rubber spatula.

7 Dissolve the gelatin in 3 oz. of boiling water; whisk into the chocolate mixture.

8 Fold in the whipped cream.

9 Pour the mousse into a 12 × 4-inch loaf pan and refrigerate.

10 *To make the chocolate spongecake*: Whip the eggs and sugar over boiling water until light and foamy.

11 Continue whipping with an electric mixer until mixture is cool and doubled in volume.

12 Sift together the flour and cocoa; fold into egg mixture with a rubber spatula.

13 Line a baking pan with parchment paper. Spread the batter to a thickness of about 1 inch over the paper.

14 Bake in a preheated 350°F oven until the cake springs back to the touch; cool on a rack.

15 Cut the spongecake into a rectangle, the size of the loaf pan; lay it on the chocolate mousse in the pan.

In recipes when the temperature is indicated, it means you should always preheat the oven for about 10 to 15 minutes so that the oven is hot or the right temperature when needed.

When you open the door of a gas oven to check the progress of the dish you are preparing, gas heat escapes very quickly and easily. Electric ovens hold their heat better, allowing heat to escape less quickly.

16 Sprinkle the raspberry liqueur over the spongecake. Refrigerate overnight.

17 *To assemble*: Dip the loaf pan briefly into hot water and invert over a wire rack; tap the mould until the mousse falls out with the sponge on the bottom.

18 Pour the melted chocolate over the terrine and spread evenly with a metal spatula. Trim off excess chocolate; refrigerate. Serve chilled on a platter. (Color photo on page T.)

White Chocolate Mousse Terrine

Yields 1 × 1½ quart cassata mould

Petits Fours Baumkuchen (page 146)

for MOUSSE

6 oz.	white chocolate
2	egg whites
2 oz.	sugar
8 oz.	heavy cream
¾ oz.	unflavored gelatin

1 Prepare the Baumkuchen Petits Fours but do not glaze with the fondant. Cool completely before cutting.

2 Cut the cake into ¼-inch-wide strips. Line the cassata mould with the strips, reserving the remaining strips for the top.

3 *For the mousse*: Chop the white chocolate and place in a bowl; melt over hot, not boiling water. Place in a large bowl.

4 In a bowl, whip the egg whites and sugar to make a meringue with soft peaks.

5 Whip the heavy cream in another bowl until soft peaks form; set aside.

6 Dissolve the gelatin in 3 oz. boiling water.

7 Whisk the meringue into the melted white chocolate. Immediately whisk in the dissolved gelatin.

8 Fold in the whipped cream with a rubber spatula.

9 Pour the mousse into the prepared cassata mould, spreading evenly. Top with the remaining cake strips.

10 Refrigerate overnight.

11 *To serve*: Unmould onto a chilled platter. (Color photo on page T.)

Almond Cream

2 oz.	blanched almonds, sliced
16 oz.	milk
6	egg yolks
3 oz.	sugar
16 oz.	heavy cream

1 Toast the almonds in an oven at 325°F until golden.

2 Heat the milk in a saucepan. Whisk together yolks and sugar in a bowl. Whisking constantly, pour the boiling milk into the yolks and sugar.

3 Stir in the almonds. Cool the mixture.

4 In a bowl, whip the cream to make soft peaks. Fold into the cooled cream. Pour mixture into 5 serving glasses. Refrigerate until ready to serve.

Mocha Mousse Terrine

Serves 8

for MOUSSE

5	egg yolks	4 oz.	cold water
4 oz.	sugar	½ oz.	instant coffee
1 oz.	unflavored gelatin	16 oz.	heavy cream

for SPONGECAKE LAYER

2	eggs	2 oz.	all-purpose flour,
1½ oz.	sugar		sifted

for GANACHE

4 oz.　semisweet chocolate　4 oz.　heavy cream

for DECORATION

4 oz.　milk chocolate

1　*To prepare the mousse*: In a bowl, whip the egg yolks and sugar until pale and fluffy.

2　In a small bowl, sprinkle the gelatin into the 4 oz. of cold water; the gelatin will absorb the water and resemble a spongy, thick mass. Place it over a saucepan of boiling water and stir until dissolved and warm to the touch. Stir in the instant coffee.

3　Whip the cream in a mixer until soft peaks form.

4　Pour the gelatin mixture into the whipped egg yolks. Continue whipping until smooth.

5　With a rubber spatula, fold the whipped cream into the egg mixture.

6　Pour the mousse into a 12 × 4-inch loaf pan. Refrigerate for about 5 to 6 hours or overnight until set.

7　*To make the spongecake layer*: Whip the 2 eggs with the 1½ oz. of sugar until thick.

8　Fold in the flour, using a rubber spatula.

9　Spread batter on a 9 × 11-inch baking sheet lined with parchment.

10　Bake in a preheated 350°F oven until golden brown and the spongecake springs back when touched.

11　Cool completely on a rack.

12　*For the ganache*: Chop the chocolate and place in a bowl. Melt the chocolate over hot, not boiling, water.

13　Pour the cream into a small saucepan and heat; the cream does not have to boil.

14 Whisk the cream into the melted chocolate and stir until completely smooth. Let cool for 1 hour.

15 *To assemble*: cut the spongecake into a 12 × 4-inch rectangle.

16 Spread half of the cooled *ganache* over the sponge in a smooth layer.

17 Unmould the mousse by dipping the mould briefly in hot water and inverting it on a board or counter.

18 Cut the mousse diagonally in half, lengthwise, to make 2 triangles.

19 Turn the halves so that they form a pyramid. Before sandwiching them together, spread the remaining *ganache* on the 2 sides that touch. Then press together to seal. Lay the pyramid on the spongecake, trimming the sides to make it even. Refrigerate while tempering the decoration.

20 *For the decoration*: Melt the milk chocolate over hot, not boiling, water. Temper the chocolate, following the directions, "To temper chocolate" (page 143).

21 Pour the tempered chocolate evenly over the pyramid, letting it run down the sides. Using a spatula, cover the entire mousse. Refrigerate.

22 Trim off excess chocolate. Serve on a platter. (Color photo on page T.)

Chestnut Mousse

Serves 6

½ oz.	unflavored gelatin	24 oz.	heavy cream
6	egg yolks	12 oz.	chestnuts, broken in pieces
2 oz.	sugar		
21 oz.	unsweetened canned chestnut purée	1 oz.	Kirsch liqueur

1 Dissolve gelatin in ⅓ cup boiling water.

2 In a large bowl, beat the yolks and sugar until pale and the mixture forms ribbons when dropped from a spoon. Add the dissolved gelatin. Fold in the purée.

3 In another bowl, whip the cream until soft peaks form.

4 Add the chestnuts and Kirsch to the egg-yolk mixture.

5 Fold in the whipped cream.

6 Turn into a mould and refrigerate overnight.

7 *To serve*: Unmould onto a chilled serving platter. Serve cold.

Coffee English Cream

> 8 oz. milk
> 8 oz. heavy cream
> 6 oz. sugar
> 2 oz. ground coffee (not instant)
> 12 egg yolks, at room temperature

1 Combine the first 4 ingredients in a saucepan; over low heat, bring to a boil. Simmer gently for 30 minutes. Bring to a full boil.

2 Beat yolks into boiling liquid. Allow to thicken. Remove from heat. To cool, pour into top of a bain-marie with ice water on the bottom.

3 When cool, refrigerate. Serve chilled.

Double Chocolate Cake

Serves 12

for CHOCOLATE SPONGECAKE

10 oz.   unsalted butter
10 oz.   semisweet chocolate
10   egg yolks
10 oz.   sugar
5   egg whites

for CHOCOLATE CREAM

8 oz.   heavy cream
½ oz.   sugar
2 oz.   semisweet chocolate

1   *To make the chocolate spongecake*: Melt the butter and chocolate over boiling water.

2   In a bowl, whip the egg yolks with 2 oz. of the sugar until pale in color. Whisk the butter-chocolate mixture into the egg yolks and sugar.

3   Whip the egg whites with the remaining 8 oz. of sugar to make a meringue with firm peaks. Using a rubber spatula, fold the meringue into the batter.

4   Butter and flour a 10 × 3-inch cake pan. Pour the batter into the prepared pan and bake in a preheated 350°F oven for 35 to 40 minutes or until a toothpick inserted in the middle comes out clean.

5   Invert cake on a wire rack and cool completely.

6   *For the chocolate cream*: Whisk together the heavy cream and sugar until soft peaks form.

7   Melt the chocolate over hot, not boiling, water. Whisk the heavy cream into the chocolate until smooth. Refrigerate.

8   Slice the cooled cake horizontally into thirds, using a serrated knife.

9   *To decorate*: Use two-thirds of the chocolate cream for the filling—divided between the cake layers. Use the remaining chocolate cream on the outside of the cake, on the top and sides.

10   Using a pastry bag fitted with a no. 1 tip, pipe rosettes on the border of the cake top. Cut cake into 12 servings.

Need to make a cake in a half hour? Always have 1 or 2 sponge-cakes in your freezer, tightly wrapped; they last for weeks. Just take them out and cut them into 3 or 4 layers with a serrated knife. With a brush, soak the layers with some syrup and sweet liqueur. Fill the layers with your favorite cream—ganache, whipped cream, or shortcake filling. Garnish with some fruit.

Windows' Chocolate Sabayon Cake

Serves 12

for SPONGECAKE

6	eggs
6 oz.	granulated sugar
3 oz.	all-purpose flour
1½ oz.	cornstarch
1½ oz.	unsweetened cocoa

for SABAYON FILLING

5	egg yolks
2 oz.	sugar
4 oz.	dry sherry
4 oz.	semisweet chocolate
1 oz.	unflavored gelatin
4 oz.	cool water
11 oz.	heavy cream
1 oz.	powdered sugar
2 oz.	chocolate shavings for garnish

1   *To make the spongecake*: Butter three 10-inch round pans and dust lightly with flour. Preheat the oven to 350°F.

2   Whip the eggs and granulated sugar together until pale.

3   Sift together the flour, cornstarch, and cocoa. Fold the sifted dry ingredients into the eggs and sugar. Pour batter into the 3 prepared pans.

4   Bake at 350°F for 30 to 40 minutes until done. Cool on a rack.

5   *For the sabayon filling*: Heat the yolks, sugar, and sherry in the top of a double boiler, whipping constantly for about 15 minutes, until light.

6   Melt the chocolate in a cup over hot, not boiling, water.

7   Dissolve gelatin in the 4 oz. of water. Then heat over a double boiler to fully dissolve. Whisk the gelatin into the yolk mixture; then whisk in the melted chocolate.

8   In a bowl, whip the cream with powdered sugar until soft peaks form. Fold into the egg mixture. Refrigerate until the sabayon sets.

9   *To assemble the cake*: Spread the sabayon filling between layers and on top and sides. Garnish with the chocolate shavings. Refrigerate until ready to serve. (Color photo on page T.)

All temperatures given in recipes for roasting are based on regular stoves and ovens. If you use an older electric range, increase the temperature by 15°F.

Chocolate Charlotte

Serves 8

8	egg yolks
6 oz.	sugar
12 oz.	milk, scalded
1½ oz.	unflavored gelatin
3 oz.	Grand Marnier liqueur or cold water
6 oz.	semisweet chocolate, melted
12 oz.	heavy cream, whipped
16	ladyfingers
4 oz.	sweetened whipped cream for garnish
2 oz.	shaved chocolate for garnish

1 Beat together the egg yolks and sugar until light. Slowly add the scalded milk, beating constantly. Cook, stirring over low flame until mixture coats a spoon; do not boil. Remove from heat.

2 Soften the gelatin in liqueur or water and heat in a small saucepan until gelatin is just dissolved. Stir gelatin into the melted chocolate and add to the egg mixture. Cool to room temperature.

3 Fold in the whipped cream. Refrigerate the charlotte cream while preparing the mould.

4 Line the bottom of a 1½-quart charlotte mould with waxed paper. Next, line the bottom and sides of the mould with ladyfingers cut to fit. Pour the charlotte cream into the lined mould and cover with plastic wrap. Refrigerate for several hours or overnight.

5 Unmould and decorate with whipped cream and shaved chocolate.

Chocolate Cake

Serves 12

12 oz.	semisweet chocolate
12 oz.	unsalted butter
12	egg yolks
12 oz.	sugar
12	egg whites
2 oz.	cocoa, for garnish

1 Melt the chocolate and butter together in top of a double boiler.

2 In a large bowl, whip the yolks with 9 oz. of the sugar. Fold the chocolate-butter mixture into the yolks.

Monter: To add cream or butter to a sauce while stirring constantly.

Spoons: Slotted spoon (stainless steel); long-handled spoon; wooden spoons.

3 In another bowl, whip the whites with the remaining sugar until soft peaks form. Fold the whites into the chocolate mixture.

4 Pour the mousse into 2 buttered and paper-lined 10-inch pans, reserving some of the mousse to cover the cakes when garnishing.

5 Bake in a preheated 250°F oven for 30 minutes; then turn oven off; leave cakes in the oven for 30 minutes. Remove from the oven and cool the cakes in the pans.

6 Unmould on 2 plates and chill the cakes in the refrigerator.

7 *To garnish*: Trim top of cakes evenly. Invert one cake on a cardboard cut the same size. Cover the cake with a thin layer of the reserved mousse. Then place the second layer on top. Smooth the remaining mousse over the top with a rubber spatula. Sprinkle with the cocoa. Cut into 12 servings.

Hazelnut Dacquoise

Serves 12 (1 10-inch cake)

for MERINGUE LAYERS

6 oz.	egg whites
1 lb.	sugar
½ lb.	toasted hazelnuts, skinned and ground

for FILLING

15 oz.	Butter Cream (recipe follows)
2 oz.	amaretto
1 oz.	strong espresso coffee, cooled

1 *For the meringue layers*: Using an electric mixer on high speed, whip the egg whites until foamy; gradually add the sugar. Continue whipping until stiff. Fold in the hazelnuts with a rubber spatula.

2 Fit a pastry bag with a no. 3 plain tip; fill the bag and pipe the meringue in three 10-inch circles onto a greased and floured baking sheet.

3 Bake at 200 to 225°F for about 1 hour until firm, dry, and lightly browned. Remove layers from the baking sheets and cool.

4 *For the filling*: Mix the Butter Cream, amaretto, and coffee. Spread the filling on each layer, stacking the layers as you work.

5 Trim the edges with a serrated knife to make straight sides (save the trimmings). Spread the filling around the sides, leaving the top bare.

6 Chop the crumbs from the trimmings and press onto the sides of the cake.

Butter Cream

Yields 15 oz.

10 oz.	unsalted butter, softened
4 oz.	sugar
2	eggs
2	egg whites

1 Whip the butter with 2½ oz. of the sugar. Add the whole eggs, one at a time. Continue whipping for 15 to 20 minutes until almost white in color.

2 In another bowl, whip the egg whites with the remaining sugar until medium peaks form. Fold into whipped butter mixture.

3 Wrap unused portion tightly and store in refrigerator.

Amaretto Cheesecake

Serves 12 (1 10-inch cake)

for LINZER DOUGH   **(yields one 10-inch pastry disc)**

3 oz.	*unsalted butter, softened*
3 oz.	*sugar*
3 oz.	*all-purpose flour*
2 oz.	*hazelnuts, ground*
½	*lemon, grated for the zest*

for CHEESECAKE

10 oz.	*Philadelphia cream cheese*
11 oz.	*sugar*
5 oz.	*sour cream*
3½ oz.	*heavy cream*
5 oz.	*milk*
4 oz.	*amaretto*
5	*eggs*

1 *To make the dough*: In a bowl, combine the butter with the sugar and flour; stir until mixed. Add the nuts and lemon zest.

2 On a board lightly dusted with flour, roll out the dough into a 10-inch round shape.

3 Lightly butter a 10-inch round cake pan. Place the dough in the bottom. Bake in a preheated 325°F oven for about 8 minutes or until dry to the touch.

4 *To make the cheesecake*: In an electric mixer, whip the cream cheese for about 5 minutes until light. Add the sugar and whip another 5 minutes. Turn machine off and scrape down sides of the bowl.

5 Add the liquids gradually, stopping machine occasionally to scrape sides of bowl.

6 Add the eggs, one at a time, beating well after each addition. Pour into a 10-inch round pan lined with the baked linzer dough. Place in a water bath and bake in a 300°F oven for 1¼ hours or until firm in the middle.

7 *Final assembly*: Allow the cheesecake to cool for several hours in the refrigerator before unmoulding. To unmould, run a sharp paring knife around the edges; invert the cake over a plate and tap against the table to unmould. Place a serving platter over the cheesecake and invert again with the cookie crust down. Cut into 12 slices.

Pastry shells, hippen shells, and barquettes can be used to garnish a plate beautifully when filled with mousse or vegetables. They can be used for hors d'oeuvres, filled with liver mousse or crunchy vegetables. Hippen shells can be filled with ice cream, sorbet, or fruit coulis.

Viennese
Apple Strudel

Serves 12

for DOUGH

16 oz.	all-purpose flour
1	egg
pinch	salt
1 oz.	vegetable oil
	lukewarm water, as needed

for FILLING

3 oz.	sweet or white bread crumbs
4 oz.	butter, melted
4½ lb.	Granny Smith or sour apples, peeled and thinly sliced
1⅓ oz.	yellow raisins
¼ oz.	ground cinnamon
3 oz.	granulated sugar
	powdered sugar

Cinnamon: The inner bark of a tree of the laurel family. A native of Ceylon and other parts of tropical Asia.

1 *To mix the dough*: Place flour on a board and make a well in the middle. Combine the egg, salt, and oil in the well. Mix with your fingertips, gradually blending in the flour. Add water in small amounts until all the flour is mixed in and the dough is smooth. Knead vigorously for 5 to 7 minutes.

2 *To roll the dough*: Spread a large soft cloth on the kitchen table and lightly dust with flour. With a rolling pin, roll out the dough on the floured cloth. Work it from the middle outwards until paper thin, lifting and turning frequently to prevent it from sticking.

3 *For the filling*: Sprinkle the bread crumbs into the 2 oz. of butter in a small pan, stirring constantly, until golden. Sprinkle the dough with the bread crumbs. Along the edge nearest you, place a thick layer of apples. Sprinkle with raisins, cinnamon, and the granulated sugar.

4 To roll, raise the cloth to lift one short end and roll up the strudel firmly, completely enclosing the apples.

5 Lift the strudel with the cloth and place on a buttered baking sheet. Remove the cloth.

6 Brush the strudel with the remaining butter. Bake at 350°F for 30 minutes or until golden brown. Dust with powdered sugar.

7 Serve warm with English Cream (page 62), whipped cream on the top, or with cream on the side. (Color photo on page V.)

Frozen Ginger Soufflé

Serves 8

¼ oz.	*fresh ginger, peeled*
4 oz.	*dry white wine*
5	*egg yolks*
7 oz.	*sugar*
3	*egg whites*
2 oz.	*superfine sugar*
3 oz.	*crystallized ginger, chopped*
16 oz.	*heavy cream, whipped*
4 oz.	*heavy cream, whipped, for garnish*

1 Grate the fresh ginger and mix with the wine in a saucepan. Boil until reduced by half. Strain and reserve the liquid.

2 In the top of a double boiler, mix the yolks, sugar, and a few drops of water. Whisk vigorously over hot, not boiling water, until light and foamy.

3 Whip egg whites with the superfine sugar until they form soft peaks.

4 Add the reserved ginger-wine liquid to the yolks. Fold in the whipped whites and cream, and 2 oz. of the chopped crystallized ginger.

5 Pour into 1 large or 8 individual soufflé moulds, fitted with a paper collar. Freeze overnight.

6 When ready to serve, remove the paper collar. Decorate the soufflé with whipped cream and remaining crystallized ginger.

Tropical Fruit Soup

Serves 8

	Syrup (recipe follows)
2	*star fruits*
3	*passion fruits*
1	*medium mango*
1	*papaya*
4	*guavas or 1 pineapple*
2	*kiwi fruits*
20	*fresh mint leaves*

1 Prepare and cool syrup before preparing the fruits.

This Tropical Fruit Soup (color photo, page u) is a dessert. When you serve a hot dessert, you could also serve this "soup" as a second one. Nearly all tropical fruits can be used if they are not too soft.

Syrup

32 oz.	*water*
8 oz.	*sugar*
10	*fresh mint leaves*
1	*lime, sliced*
1	*orange, sliced*
½	*vanilla bean*
¹⁄₁₆ oz.	*fresh ginger, thinly sliced*
½	*lemon rind, chopped*
4	*coriander seeds*
1	*whole clove*

1 Mix all ingredients in a saucepan and bring to a boil; set aside to cool.

2 Strain syrup when cool. Refrigerate till you use.

2   Wash, peel, and, if necessary, core the fruit.

3   Thinly and decoratively slice the fruits so that they have an attractive appearance.

4   Pour the chilled syrup over the fruit and marinate for 2 hours in the refrigerator. Serve in soup plates. Garnish with mint leaves.

Sangria Savarin with Fresh Fruits

Serves 10

for SAVARIN

⅓ oz.	*fresh or compressed yeast*
1 oz.	*lukewarm water*
3½ oz.	*all-purpose flour*
2¼ oz.	*unsalted butter, at room temperature*
½ oz.	*sugar*
1	*egg*
dash	*salt*

for FRUIT GARNISH

3 oz.	*fresh blackberries*
3 oz.	*fresh strawberries*
20	*fresh mint leaves*
30	*orange segments*
30	*grapefruit segments*
	Sangria Syrup (recipe follows)

1   *To make the savarin*: Dissolve yeast in the lukewarm water with one-third of the flour; combine to form a paste. Let rise in a warm place, covered with a damp towel, for 15 minutes.

2   Add the butter, sugar, and remaining flour to the yeast mixture; add the egg and mix to form a smooth paste.

3   Rub some butter on 10 ring moulds with a 3-inch diameter. Divide the paste into 10 parts and press into the moulds. Let rise for 20 minutes.

4   Bake at 300°F for 15 minutes. Unmould and cool.

5   *To serve*: On individual plates, arrange the savarins filled with fruits and some Sangria Syrup on the side of the plates as a garnish.

If you use fruits in some of your recipes, buy them several days before you need them; ripen the fruits at room temperature. When they are ripe, place the fruits in the refrigerator (with the exception of bananas). Nothing is worse than unripened fruit in a recipe. Bananas taste best when the skin is light black outside. For fruit purée, sorbet, or mousse, use only overripe fruits. Then you extract the full taste.

Sangria Syrup

32 oz.	*California red wine*
1	*orange rind*
1	*lemon rind*
1	*cinnamon stick*
5	*cloves, whole*
3 oz.	*sugar*
1 oz.	*cornstarch*

1   In a saucepan, mix all the ingredients except the cornstarch. Bring to a boil. Strain.

2   Pour the hot syrup over the cool savarin; soak until the syrup cools.

3   Bring the remaining syrup to a boil; bind lightly with 1 oz. of cornstarch diluted in a little cold water. Cool; pour into a serving pitcher.

Apple Bavarian Cream

Serves 12 (1 10-inch cake)

for APPLE FILLING

16 oz.	*heavy cream*
1 oz.	*water*
1 oz.	*applejack or Calvados*
½ oz.	*unflavored gelatin*
16 oz.	*Apple Purée (recipe follows)*
1 (9-inch)	*spongecake layer (page 114)*
18	*ladyfingers*

1   *To make the filling*: Whip the cream and set aside.

2   Combine the water and applejack or Calvados in a small bowl. Sprinkle the gelatin on the surface. Allow the gelatin to stand for 5 minutes to absorb the liquid. Place the bowl over a pan of simmering water to melt the gelatin. Remove the gelatin when it is clear.

3   Place the apple purée in a bowl. Stir half a cupful into the melted gelatin. Then whip this into the remaining apple purée.

4   Fold in the whipped cream.

5   *To assemble*: Cut ¼-inch slices from the spongecake; place slices in the bottom of a 10-inch springform pan.

6   Trim the ladyfingers straight on the sides and cut the bottoms flat. Fit the ladyfingers, rounded side out, tightly close together between the spongecake and the inside of the springform.

7   Pour in the filling. Chill for several hours or overnight to set the filling.

8   Run a heated knife blade around the edges of the pan. Unmould onto a serving platter. Cut into 12 portions. Serve cold.

Apple Purée

2 lbs.	*Golden Delicious apples*
4 oz.	*water*
6 oz.	*sugar*
½	*lemon, squeezed for the juice*
pinch	*ground cinnamon*

1   Peel, core, and thinly slice the apples.

2   Place in a saucepan with the remaining ingredients and cook over medium heat, stirring occasionally, until water evaporates and apples are thickened. Cool the apple mixture.

3   Purée the apple mixture in a food processor.

Golden Lemon Tart

Serves 6 to 8 (1 9-inch pie)

for BAKED PIECRUST

6 oz.	*all-purpose flour*
pinch	*salt*
4 oz.	*unsalted butter or shortening, chilled and cut into small pieces*
2 oz.	*cold water*

for FILLING

¼ oz.	cornstarch
12 oz.	water
5	egg yolks
4 oz.	fresh lemon juice, strained
4 oz.	sugar
1 oz.	unsalted butter
¼ oz.	unflavored gelatin
4 oz.	heavy cream, whipped
4	dry Italian macaroons (amaretti), crushed
2 oz.	apricot jam
2	large lemons, thinly sliced

1 *To make the piecrust*: In a bowl, mix the flour and salt with the butter by rubbing with your palms until the mixture resembles cornmeal. Make a well and pour the water into the well; mix by hand until the dough forms a ball. (This should happen very quickly; do not overwork). Chill the dough for 20 to 30 minutes.

2 Lightly flour a working surface and a rolling pin. Roll out the dough until ¼-inch thick. Line a 9-inch quiche pan or flan ring with the dough, pressing it into the corners and sides. Chill for 20 minutes.

3 Line the unbaked pastry with aluminum foil; fill with dried beans or rice.

4 Bake the pastry at 350°F for about 25 minutes until the crust is golden brown. Remove the beans or rice and foil; cool the pastry.

5 *To make the filling*: Dissolve cornstarch in 2 oz. of the water. Add the egg yolks and mix thoroughly; set aside.

6 In a saucepan, combine the lemon juice, 5 oz. of the water, and sugar. Bring to a boil. Add 2 oz. of the hot liquid to the yolk mixture, stirring constantly. Next, add the yolk mixture to the hot lemon mixture and continue stirring. Return to the heat and boil for 3 minutes. Remove from the heat and stir in the butter. Cool the lemon mixture and refrigerate.

7 Over boiling water, dissolve the gelatin in 3 oz. of the water. Fold the gelatin into the cold lemon mixture, mixing thoroughly. Fold in the whipped cream and add the crushed macaroons.

8 Fill the baked piecrust with the lemon mixture.

9 In a small pan, melt the jam with the remaining water to make a glaze; keep warm. Dip the lemon slices in the glaze.

10 *To garnish*: Starting from the outside edge, cover the top with the glazed lemon slices.

APPELLATION SAUTERNES CONTROLÉE

Château d'Yquem
Lur-Saluces
— 1971 —
MIS EN BOUTEILLE AU CHATEAU
CM Christian Murat

Apple Pancake Tart

Serves 10 (7 pancakes per person)

for PANCAKE		
	3½ oz.	all-purpose flour
	1	egg yolk
	2	eggs
	12 oz.	milk
	pinch	salt
	4 oz.	vegetable oil

for APPLE AND ALMOND FILLING		
	5	Granny Smith apples
	1½ oz.	unsalted butter
	3 oz.	granulated sugar
	2 oz.	Calvados
	3½ oz.	unsalted butter
	2 oz.	sugar
	2	egg yolks
	3	egg whites
	2 oz.	ground almonds
	2 oz.	all-purpose flour

for GLAZE	
	apricot marmalade
	blanched almonds, sliced
	powdered sugar

1 *To make the pancakes*: In a bowl, combine all the pancake ingredients except the vegetable oil; mix to form a smooth batter.

2 Heat a 7-inch skillet and brush lightly with the oil.

3 Pour in a little batter, tilting pan so that it runs all over; cook over medium heat until bubbles appear on the surface. Turn pancake over and cook on the other side for half a minute.

4 Transfer pancake to a plate. Continue with remaining batter; be careful not to make the pancakes too thick.

5 Cool all the pancakes completely before layering with the filling.

6 *For the filling*: Peel, core, and cut each apple into 8 wedges.

7 In a skillet, melt the 1½ oz. of butter; add the sugar and cook until carmelized. Stir in the apple wedges and cook briefly. Add the Calvados and continue cooking another minute or two; cool the apples.

8 Whip butter and sugar in a bowl until smooth; add the yolks and continue whipping until pale and fluffy.

9 In another bowl, whip the egg whites and sugar until smooth peaks form. Fold egg whites into the butter mixture, using a rubber spatula.

10 Combine the almonds and flour; fold gently into the egg mass.

11 *To assemble the tart*: Place a pancake on a baking sheet lined with parchment paper. Arrange apple wedges in an even layer over the pancake. Top with some almond filling. (Reserve a small amount of the almond filling for the outside.) For the next layer, add another pancake, apples, and filling. Continue in this manner until all the apples and pancakes are used. Smooth the remaining filling all over the outside of the tart. Bake in a preheated 350°F oven for 30 minutes or until golden brown.

12 *To glaze*: Remove from the oven and spread the apricot marmalade smoothly over the hot tart. Arrange sliced almonds all over the top and sides. Sprinkle completely with powdered sugar. Place the tart under a preheated broiler for 2 or 3 minutes or until caramelized.

13 *To serve*: Pour a little Cinnamon Sauce (recipe follows) on each plate. Place a slice of the tart on the sauce. Garnish with apple wedges.

Apple Tart with Almonds

Serves 6

4 oz.	*unsalted butter, chilled and cut into small cubes*
6 oz.	*all-purpose flour*
2 oz.	*ice water*
6	*Golden Delicious apples*
4 oz.	*butter, melted*
2 oz.	*sugar*
4 oz.	*almonds, sliced*
4 oz.	*heavy cream, whipped, for garnish*

1 *To make the piecrust*: Rub the chilled butter into the flour, leaving pieces of butter the size of walnuts. (This piecrust may be made in a food processor, using the on and off strokes.)

2 Add the ice water and mix to a paste. Cover dough and refrigerate for half an hour.

3 Roll the piecrust into 6 discs, about 4 inches in diameter and ¼-inch thick. Place on a buttered baking sheet.

4 *To prepare the apples*: Peel and core the apples; cut in half and thinly slice. Arrange sliced apples on top of the piecrust.

5 Brush with the melted and sprinkle a few almonds and a teaspoon of sugar on each.

6 Bake the tarts at 400°F for 10 to 15 minutes until golden brown. Garnish with whipped cream.

Cinnamon Sauce

4 oz.	*milk*
4 oz.	*heavy cream*
1	*cinnamon stick*
2 oz.	*sugar*
3	*egg yolks*

1 Combine the milk and cream in a medium saucepan, add the cinnamon stick and bring to a boil.

2 In a bowl, whip the yolks and sugar until pale in color.

3 Slowly whisk the hot milk into the beaten yolks; pour back into the saucepan.

4 Return the mixture to a low burner and heat, stirring continuously until thickened; do not boil. Serve at room temperature.

Pecan Diamonds

Yields about 75 diamonds

for PECANS

8 oz.	unsalted butter
4 oz.	honey
8 oz.	light brown sugar
1 lb.	pecan pieces
2 oz.	heavy cream

for COOKIE DOUGH

3 oz.	sugar
6 oz.	unsalted butter, softened
9 oz.	all-purpose flour
1	egg

1 *To prepare the pecans*: In a saucepan, mix the butter, honey, and brown sugar over low heat.

2 Add the pecans and cream, blending well.

3 *To make the cookie dough*: In an electric mixer, combine all the cookie ingredients. Roll out and spread on a 9 × 13-inch baking sheet lined with waxed paper.

4 Spread the pecan mixture over the cookie dough.

5 Bake at 375°F for 20 to 30 minutes or until bubbly.

6 Cool completely (preferably overnight in the refrigerator); cut into diamonds.

Sugared Fried Walnuts

Serves 8

3	egg whites
2 oz.	cornstarch
8 oz.	walnut halves, shelled
6 oz.	powdered sugar
16 oz.	vegetable oil, for frying

1 In a bowl, lightly beat the egg whites with the cornstarch; the mixture should be runny.

2 Dip the walnut halves into the whites; scrape off the excess.

3 Dip the walnuts, one by one, into the sugar.

4 In a medium saucepan, heat the oil over medium heat. One at a time, drop the walnuts into the hot oil; fry until golden. Transfer to paper towels; cool.

5 Arrange on a serving platter or make in advance and store in a covered container. (Color photo on page W.)

Weinbeisser

for GLAZE

3 oz.	granulated sugar
1½ oz.	water
3	egg whites
8 oz.	granulated sugar

for DOUGH

8 oz.	honey
8 oz.	all-purpose flour
1	egg
½ oz.	baking soda
½ oz.	gingerbread seasoning (in specialty stores)
dash	ground nutmeg
dash	white pepper, freshly ground
28 oz.	all-purpose flour

1 *To make the glaze*: bring the 3 oz. of sugar and the water to a boil in a saucepan; set aside.

2 Whip the egg whites and the 8 oz. of sugar over a low heat into a warm mixture, do not overheat. Remove from heat and whip until cool.

3 Add the boiled sugar mixture to the whipped egg-white mixture, mixing until combined mixtures becomes more liquefied in consistency. Set aside until needed.

4 *To prepare the dough*: Honey should be room temperature. Mix with the 8 oz. of flour; cover and let rest in a cool place for 2 days.

5 Whip the egg with the baking soda and gingerbread spices; then mix with the rested dough. Add the remaining flour.

6 Roll out to ¼-inch thickness; cut into 1½-inch circles. Dip top into the glaze and place onto a wire rack. Let sugar dry for about 1 hour. Then place onto a baking sheet.

7 Bake in a preheated 325°F oven for 20 to 25 minutes. Cool on a rack. (Color photo on page W.)

Keep these tasty cookies in your favorite cookie jar! Serve at a wine party. The sweetness of the cookie blends delightfully with the acidity of the wine.

Nutmeg: The kernel of the fruit of the Myristica tree grown in the East Indies. The whole fruit resembles an apricot.

Dried Fruits in Filo with Apricot Sorbet

Serves 8

6 oz.	mixed dried fruits (banana chips, pineapple rings, apricots, figs, dates, raisins, apples, and others)
3 oz.	Simple Syrup (page 63)
1 oz.	apricot brandy

for HAZELNUT FILLING

4 oz.	unsalted butter, at room temperature
4 oz.	sugar
2	egg yolks
2	egg whites
2 oz.	hazelnuts, roasted and ground
2 oz.	all-purpose flour
3 oz.	filo (4 leaves) approximately 8″ × 16″
2 oz.	unsalted butter, melted

for APRICOT SAUCE

	English Cream (page 62)
1 oz.	apricot brandy
	Apricot Sorbet (recipe follows)

1 *To prepare the fruits*: Chop the dried fruits into small cubes; place in a bowl.

2 Pour the Simple Syrup and apricot brandy over the fruits and mix. Let stand at room temperature for 1 to 2 hours until the fruits soften.

3 *For the hazelnut filling*: In a mixing bowl, whip the butter with 2 oz. of the sugar until pale and light. Add the 2 yolks and continue whipping until smooth.

4 In another bowl, whip the egg whites with 2 oz. of sugar until medium peaks form; the meringue should be glossy and smooth, not dry. Gently fold the meringue into the yolk mixture with a rubber spatula.

5 Sift the flour and combine it with the roasted hazelnuts. Fold into the filling; be careful not to overmix.

6 Drain the dried fruits and gently mix them into the filling. (The syrup can be used in Apricot Sorbet.) This mixture can be refrigerated overnight.

Apricot Sorbet

Serves 8

14 oz.	ripe apricots
4 oz.	water
2 oz.	sugar
1 oz.	apricot liqueur or lemon juice
1	lemon

1 In a saucepan with boiling water, blanch the apricots for 10 seconds. Remove with a skimmer and refresh in cold water for a few seconds. Peel the apricots and discard the pits; cut into quarters.

2 Add the sugar to the 4 oz. water and bring to a boil. Add the apricots and simmer for about 2 to 3 minutes. Pour into a blender and mix; set aside to cool.

3 Stir the liqueur or lemon juice into the apricot mixture. Place in a sorbet machine. Freeze until you have the desired consistency.

7 *To stuff*: Spread the strudel leaves on a dry counter; coat each with melted butter, using a pastry brush.

8 Stack 2 leaves on top of each other, making 2 piles of 2 leaves each. Cut each pile into 8 rectangles, so that you have 16.

9 Put a spoonful of filling in the middle of each rectangle. Gather the ends up, and pinch the filo together to form a little pouch.

10 Place stuffed pouches on a baking sheet lined with baking parchment. Bake in a preheated 350°F oven for about 15 minutes until golden brown. Keep warm until ready to serve.

11 *For the sauce*: Combine the English Cream with the 1 oz. of apricot brandy.

12 *Final assembly*: On the plate, serve 2 stuffed pouches, apricot sauce, and a scoop of apricot sorbet. (Color photo on page U.)

1957

"Now, you're sure this is very nice? We have an educated palate coming for dinner."

Banquets

Banquet Wines

Part of my job as wine director at Windows on the World is helping people plan menus and make wine selections for large parties. The most important point to remember is that any large gathering of people also means a variety of different tastes. The other consideration is the overall personality of the group. If the people are not highly knowledgeable about wine and food, there's no sense in buying extremely expensive wines.

Keeping these two points in mind, your goal is to find some easily drinkable red and white wines to please your guests. Rather than having an expensive Champagne, you may choose to substitute a high-quality California or a Spanish sparkling wine at a lesser price. You may also select a wine from the Mâconnais, such as a Mâcon Blanc, instead of its more expensive counterpart, Pouilly-Fuissé.

If you are most concerned about the cost of your party and you would like to save on your wine bill, no matter how tempting it looks, do not have the house wine in carafes on every table. The only time you should serve wine from a carafe is when it has been decanted, but still let your guests know what they are having with their meal. I always believe it is more elegant to have corked bottles.

To make your party progress more smoothly, get to know your banquet director. Find out if you are being charged a fixed rate for the bar. If you will be billed for each empty bottle, be sure to speak to him about instructing the waiters *not* to overpour—that is, to fill your guests' wine glasses to the rim and then top up constantly. It's annoying and wasteful.

If your group is more aware of wine and food, and you have in mind a special wine to serve—by all means, ask your banquet director. He may either have the wine on his regular list, in which case he can merely substitute your choice for his house wine, or perhaps he can order it specially for your party. Something can almost always be arranged if you discuss it in advance.

Occasionally I am asked by people, "Why can't I bring my own wines?" That's highly unusual in a restaurant situation, because it's like bringing a boxed lunch, but it does happen in rare circumstances. In this situation, the hotel or restaurant charges a corkage fee—a charge of $10 or $15 per bottle for opening the wine and serving it.

How much wine should you buy for your party? We estimate a half bottle per person. This works out to twelve ounces or two six-ounce glasses. It is an accurate estimate as long as you are using one or two wines for the party. Here's a step-by-step method to make a wine selection for your party:

1. Consider your budget.
2. Choose the food menu.
3. Choose the wine or wines, if you decide to serve a red and a white, or if you want to serve Champagne, too. If you choose a Champagne to go with your menu (or an expensive Burgundy), it may be wise to ask the banquet director to suggest a more reasonably priced substitute.

If you decide to have only one kind of wine at your party, white wine is your best bet because it's a crowd pleaser. At Windows on the World, 85 percent of our guests who have one wine at their banquet choose white.

Inexpensive Wines for Large Banquets

White Wines
Alsace Riesling
California Sauvignon Blanc
Mâcon Blanc
Pinot Grigio or Soave (Italian)

Red Wines
Cabernet Sauvignon (Beaulieu, Martini, Parducci, Simi, Pedroncelli)
Chianti
Beaujolais
Rioja (Spanish)
Petit Château (Bordeaux, France)

Sparkling Wines
California, Spanish

Sea Scallops on Cucumber

Serves 12

12	medium sea scallops
2 oz.	olive oil
½	lemon, squeezed for the juice
1	fresh basil sprig, chopped
1	fresh thyme sprig, chopped
	white pepper, freshly ground
1 pc.	European cucumber
2 oz.	Crème Fraîche (page 36)
8 oz.	fresh horseradish, grated
	salt
8 oz.	chive

1 Clean and thinly slice the scallops.

2 In a bowl, mix the oil, lemon juice, basil, thyme, and pepper to make a marinade. Add the scallops and marinate for 4 hours in the refrigerator.

3 Peel the cucumber and cut into ¼-inch slices. Scoop out the seeds without making a hole through the cucumber.

4 Whip the crème fraîche lightly in a bowl and mix with the horse-radish. Season with salt and pepper.

5 Fill the cucumber rounds with the cream. Place sliced scallops on top and sprinkle with chives. Serve chilled.

Quail Galantine with Duck Liver

Yields 10 to 12 slices (1 small terrine)

4	fresh quails
	salt
	white pepper, freshly ground
2 oz.	spinach leaves, cleaned
3 oz.	duck liver
1 oz.	vegetable oil

1 Debone the quails, starting from the back, so that the skin remains intact without holes. Season with salt and pepper.

2 Blanch the spinach; drain and dry thoroughly.

3 Clean the duck liver and sauté very quickly in oil in a very hot skillet; sauté on each side. Set aside to cool.

4 Spread out the deboned quails. Arrange the spinach on top and add a truffle slice.

5 Set duck liver on top; season with salt and pepper.

6 Roll up in buttered aluminum foil.

7 Poach in salted water for about 12 minutes. Cool in the liquid; then remove aluminum foil.

8 Cover and refrigerate overnight. Cut in ¼-inch slices before serving.

Quail Egg on Marinated Baby Artichoke Heart

		Serves 12
6	*quail eggs*	
1 oz.	*sherry vinegar*	
12	*baby artichokes*	
2	*lemons, cut*	
1	*medium carrot*	
1	*medium leek*	
¼ oz.	*sturgeon caviar*	
1	*bunch fresh flat-leaf parsley*	

1 On the previous day, cook the quail eggs in boiling water for about 8 minutes. Cool and leave eggs in cold water. Add the vinegar and store overnight in the refrigerator. (This will soften the skins, so that eggs can be peeled more easily the next day.)

2 Clean artichokes until only the hearts are left; rub with lemon and boil for about 10 minutes in salted water until still firm. Let cool in the cooking liquid.

3 Peel the carrot; clean the leek. Cut carrot and leek into fine julienne slices. Blanch in salted water for half a minute.

4 Arrange the vegetables on the artichoke hearts.

5 Peel and cut quail eggs in half; place a half in the middle of the vegetables. Top with the caviar. Garnish with parsley leaves.

To clean artichokes: Place a whole artichoke on the edge of your working table. Holding one hand on it, break the stem off with the other so that the strings are pulled out from the bottom. Trim the bottom with a small knife and cut the leaves with a serrated knife. Then rub the artichoke with lemon juice to prevent discoloration. Scoop out inedible choke with a spoon and discard. To cook: Put artichokes into boiling salted water with some lemon juice added. Cook until still firm. Remove from heat and let cool in the liquid until needed.

Marinated Salmon with Sour Cream Blinis

Yields 12 Pieces

2 oz.	unsalted butter
2 oz.	sour cream
3	egg yolks
3	egg whites
2 oz.	all-purpose flour
pinch	fine salt

for GARNISH

12 slices	dill-marinated salmon
½	cucumber
1	bunch watercress

1 Whip the butter in a bowl until pale in color. Add the sour cream and egg yolks; set aside.

2 In another bowl, whip egg whites until firm; fold in flour and salt.

3 Combine the butter mixture with the egg whites. Fill individual 1½-inch round moulds.

4 Preheat oven and bake at 350°F for 10 minutes. Remove blinis from oven and arrange on a serving platter.

5 *To garnish the blinis*: Shape the salmon slices into rosettes. Set on top of the lukewarm blinis.

6 Garnish with scooped cucumber balls and a watercress leaf. Serve at room temperature. Do not refrigerate.

Boureks with Ground Lamb

Serves 8

1 oz.	olive oil		½ oz.	tomato paste
1 oz.	onion, chopped		½ oz.	parsley, chopped
1	garlic clove, chopped		dash	ground cumin
8 oz.	finely ground lamb		dash	ground ginger
	salt		dash	ground allspice
	white pepper, freshly ground		8	filo leaves

Save marmalade jars with lids on or any other glass jars with a lid. Put fresh herbs and branches into the jar; cover and refrigerate. Fresh herbs may stay fresh from 7 to 10 days.

Allspice: The dried berry of the West Indian pimento tree. The flavor resembles nutmeg, cloves, and cinnamon.

1 Heat the oil in a skillet; add the onion and sauté for 1 minute. Add the garlic and lamb.

2 Season with salt and pepper; cook over low heat for about 5 minutes until the meat is well done.

3 Add the tomato paste and sauté for half a minute. Remove from heat and drain off the excess fat. Add the spices. Set aside to cool.

4 Wrap in filo leaves following the procedure in steps 8 to 12 of Boureks Stuffed with Sweetbreads and Mushrooms (page 25).

Stuffed Pattypan Squash with Fresh Mussels

Yields 12 pieces

12	*pattypan squash (cymling)*
1	*small zucchini*
1	*small yellow squash*
2 oz.	*olive oil*
½ oz.	*shallot, finely chopped*
1	*garlic clove, finely chopped*
3 oz.	*Tomato Concassé (page 100)*
	salt
	white pepper, freshly ground
2 oz.	*mussels, cooked, shelled and diced*
1	*fresh rosemary sprig*
1	*fresh thyme sprig*

1 In a large pot, blanch the pattypan squash in salted water for 1½ minutes. Cool in the liquid; then remove. Cut stem end off the squash and reserve for baking after filling; remove seeds and discard.

2 Cut zucchini and yellow squash into ¼-inch dice.

3 In a skillet, heat the olive oil and add the shallot and garlic; sauté for 5 seconds. Add the zucchini and yellow squash; sauté for 1 minute. Add the Tomato Concassé. Then season with salt and pepper, and add the mussels, cooking until the liquid has evaporated.

4 Add chopped rosemary and thyme to the filling.

5 Scoop the filling into each pattypan squash shell; replace the stem tops. Sprinkle with the remaining olive oil; heat in a moderate oven (350°F) for about 1 minute until just warm.

Pepper, white: Made from the remains of the fully ripened berry after the outer coat has been removed.

Rosemary: Part of the evergreen population. The leaves and flowers are used as an additional flavoring in many recipes.

Roast Loin of Veal Filled with Spinach and Pignolias

Serves 8 to 10

½	veal loin (4 lbs.)
1 lb.	spinach leaves, fresh and cleaned
1 oz.	parsley leaves
3	eggs
6 oz.	heavy cream
1 oz.	shallot, chopped
8 oz.	pignolias (pine nuts)
	salt
	white pepper, freshly ground
	nutmeg, freshly grated
16 oz.	Brown Veal Stock (page 153)

1   Trim the veal loin of excess fat and nerves. Cut off and discard all but 2½ inches of the extending flank.

2   Sauté spinach in the butter with the shallot for 2 minutes. Set aside.

3   Dice the trimmed off part of flank and grind finely with the sautéed spinach.

4   Place the ground meat-spinach mixture in a bowl. Gradually add the eggs and heavy cream. Mix by hand, adding the pignolias. Season with salt, pepper, and nutmeg.

5   Season inside of the trimmed loin with salt and pepper. Place the stuffing on the upper end of the loin. Roll the loin over towards the flat end. Tie firmly with string.

6   Season the outer side of the loin with salt. Roast for 1½ hours at 350°F until the meat is still pink inside. *Do not overcook veal.*

7   Remove from oven; place veal on platter and rest for 5 to 10 minutes. Deglaze the roasting pan with the stock and simmer for a few minutes; then strain and serve sauce on the side. Remove the strings from the veal and slice (not too thinly). (Color photo on page P.)

Roast
Beef Tenderloin
Stuffed with Morels

Serves 8

3 lbs.	beef tenderloin
12 oz.	fresh morels or 2 oz. dried morels
3 oz.	clarified unsalted butter
2 oz.	shallot, finely chopped
¼ oz.	chive, cut
¼ oz.	chervil, chopped
	salt
	white pepper, freshly ground
3 oz.	spinach leaves, washed
2 oz.	vegetable oil

1 Trim the tenderloin and cut off the ends. With a long thin knife, cut the tenderloin lengthwise to make a pocket for the stuffing.

2 Clean the morels and cut off the stems. If large, cut morels in half. If using dried morels, soak them in water for 30 minutes.

3 In a skillet, sauté the shallot in half of the butter; add the morels and sauté for half a minute. Add the herbs and season to taste with salt and pepper. Set aside to cool.

4 In a skillet, sauté the spinach with remaining half of the butter. Season and mix with the morels.

5 To stuff the tenderloin with the morels and spinach, use the handle of a wooden spoon to push the stuffing into the pocket.

6 Bind tenderloin with a cord. Season with salt and pepper.

7 In a roasting pan on top of the stove, heat the oil and brown the tenderloin on each side. Roast in a preheated 350°F oven for about 15 minutes, or only until the meat is medium rare.

8 Remove tenderloin from the pan and cool for 10 minutes before slicing. Serve 2 slices per person. (Color photo on page P.)

Serve this dish with morel sauce and Duchesse Potatoes (page 140) or Dauphinoise Potatoes (page 141) and your favorite vegetable.

Do you have plants in your home? Try to plant your favorite herbs in a plant pot. I bet they will grow!

Chive: A small perennial plant of the same genus as the leek and onion. Cultivated as a potherb.

Duchesse Potatoes

Serves 8

4	large potatoes		white pepper,
	salt		freshly ground
2	eggs	1	egg yolk
	ground nutmeg	1/16 oz.	chive, cut

1 Peel the potatoes, rinse, and cut in 1-inch cubes. Boil potatoes in salted water and drain. Place potatoes in a pan over low heat, or place in a slow oven so that the steaming potatoes will dry slightly.

2 Pass potatoes through a strainer or sieve. With a wooden spoon, mix potatoes in a bowl with the 2 eggs, salt, pepper, and nutmeg.

3 Butter a baking sheet or an ovenproof dish. Using a pastry tube with a star tip, dress potatoes in cone-shaped circles, about 2 inches high. Potatoes can be stored this way in the refrigerator until ready to bake.

4 Whip the egg yolk thoroughly. Use as an egg wash to brush the potatoes.

5 Bake in a preheated 375°F oven for about 12 to 15 minutes or until golden brown. Serve warm.

Professionally, "dress" has several meanings for a chef: 1. To arrange the food nicely on a plate; 2. to decorate a turkey or other food; 3. to bind beef tenderloin or other meat with butcher's string in order to shape the meat to be round.

Potato and Apple Gratin

Serves 8

4	large potatoes		salt
1 lb.	McIntosh apples,		white pepper,
	peeled and cored		freshly ground
10 oz.	heavy cream	1 oz.	unsalted butter

1 Peel and wash the potatoes. Slice potatoes ¼-inch thick; do not rinse potato slices in water.

2 Peel, core, and slice the apples ¼-inch thick.

3 In a bowl, mix potatoes and apples with the heavy cream and season well.

4 Place the mixture in a buttered, flat ovenproof dish. Bake in a preheated 350°F oven for about 30 minutes until nicely browned.

5 To serve, cut into 2 × 2-inch squares, using a small knife; lift from the baking dish with a spatula.

You can replace the apple in this recipe with blanched leek or you could use both.

Dauphinoise Potatoes

Serves 8

4	large potatoes		white pepper,
16 oz.	heavy cream		freshly ground
	salt	1	garlic clove
	ground nutmeg	1 oz.	unsalted butter

1 Peel and rinse potatoes; dry thoroughly.

2 Slice potatoes ⅛-inch thick. Mix with the cream and season to taste with salt, pepper, and nutmeg.

3 Rub a flat ovenproof dish with the garlic; then rub with the butter.

4 Fill the dish with the potato mixture.

5 Bake at 350°F for about 30 to 40 minutes or until the potatoes are tender and browned on top.

Soufflé Nicoise

Serves 8

20 oz.	milk	3¼ oz.	Swiss cheese, grated
	salt	6	egg whites
	white pepper,	16 oz.	Ratatouille
	freshly ground		(recipe follows)
	ground nutmeg	1 oz.	black olives,
2¼ oz.	unsalted butter		pitted and diced
3	eggs	1 oz.	unsalted butter
5	egg yolks		for ramekins
2¼ oz.	all-purpose flour	1 oz.	all-purpose flour
1 oz.	cornstarch		for ramekins

1 Season the milk with salt, pepper, and nutmeg. Bring three-quarters of the milk to a boil in a large saucepan.

2 In a bowl, mix the eggs and egg yolks, flour, and cornstarch with the remaining cold milk. Slowly add to the boiling milk; turn heat down to very low and cook, stirring constantly. When the mixture thickens into a thick custard, remove from the heat and stir in the cheese; cool.

3 Beat the egg whites until stiff. Fold into the cool custard.

4 Carefully fold in the finely cut Ratatouille and olives. Butter and lightly flour sixteen 2-inch ramekins and fill with the mixture.

5 Bake at 350°F for about 25 minutes until golden and puffy. Serve immediately.

Ratatouille

Yields 16 oz.

3 oz.	eggplant
3 oz.	zucchini
2 oz.	red bell pepper
2 oz.	green bell pepper
4 oz.	onion
3 oz.	olive oil
	salt
	pepper, freshly ground
3	garlic cloves, chopped
1	fresh thyme sprig

1 Dice the vegetables into ¼-inch pieces.

2 Sauté the vegetables *separately* in olive oil for 2 minutes.

3 Combine the vegetables and seasonings in one pan; simmer for 2 minutes and correct the seasonings.

Cheese Fours Swans

for SWANS   **Yields 25 swans**

Pâte à Choux for Cheese Fours (recipe follows)

for FILLING

7 oz.	Philadelphia cream cheese	pepper
2 oz.	Crème Fraîche (page 36)	fresh parsley, chopped
	salt	optional herbs

1 Line a baking sheet with parchment. Pipe two-thirds of the Pâte à Choux with a no. 2 star tip into teardrop shapes onto the parchment. Use the remaining pâte for the swan necks, piping thin "S" shapes with a no. 1 straight tip.

2 Bake at 350°F for 15 to 20 minutes until golden. Cool.

3 With a wooden spoon, combine the cream cheese and crème fraîche just until mixed. Add salt, pepper, parsley, and whatever herbs you prefer.

4 Slice teardrop puffs in half horizontally with a serrated knife.

5 Pipe a mound of filling into the bottom half. Cut top portion in half and secure on the cream cheese to resemble swan wings.

6 Add the necks, pushing into the cream cheese to secure. Arrange on a serving platter. (Color photo on page W.)

Cheese Savories

Yields about 46 pieces

3½ oz.	unsalted butter, softened	1	egg yolk
			salt
3½ oz.	Edam, Parmesan or Romano cheese, grated		white pepper, freshly ground
7 oz.	all-purpose flour	pinch	paprika
40	walnut halves	1	egg

1 Combine the softened butter with the grated cheese, flour, egg yolk, salt, pepper, and paprika to form a dough.

2 Roll to ¼-inch thickness. Using a cookie cutter, cut into 2-inch rounds. Whip the egg for an egg wash; brush on top of each round.

3 Arrange on a baking sheet lined with parchment. Place one walnut half on each round. Bake at 350°F for 8 to 10 minutes until golden brown. Serve warm. (Color photo on page W.)

Pâte à Choux for Cheese Fours

4¼ oz. milk
2¼ oz. unsalted butter
½ oz. sugar
dash salt
2¾ oz. all-purpose flour
2 eggs
chive, finely cut
fresh parsley, finely chopped

1 In a casserole, bring the milk, butter, sugar, and salt to a boil. Add the flour and mix with a wooden spoon until mixture loosens from the side of casserole. Add the herbs and set aside to cool off, stirring occasionally.

2 Add the eggs, one by one, stirring to incorporate each.

3 Mixture can be refrigerated overnight. Use as directed in the recipe.

Paprika: A sweet red pepper, which is dried and ground after the seeds and stems are removed.

Chocolate Truffles Milk Chocolate Almond

Yields 10 truffles

8 oz.	*milk chocolate*
6 oz.	*heavy cream*
2 oz.	*Crème Fraîche (page 36)*
2oz.	*almonds, ground and roasted*

for DECORATION

12 oz.	*milk chocolate*
1 oz.	*ground almonds, roasted*

1 *To make the truffles*: Chop the 8 oz. of milk chocolate; melt on top of a double boiler over hot, not boiling, water.

2 In a small saucepan, heat the heavy cream and crème fraîche together.

3 Whisk the hot cream into the melted chocolate.

4 Stir in the almonds. Tightly wrap and refrigerate the mixture for 1 to 2 hours.

5 Using a pastry bag fitted with a no. 5 plain tip, pipe 1-inch balls onto a sheet of parchment. Place in freezer for 15 to 20 minutes.

6 Remove from refrigerator to shape truffles. Between the palms of the hands, roll each ball into a smooth round shape. Freeze again until milk chocolate coating is tempered.

7 *To temper chocolate*: Chop the 12 oz. of milk chocolate, and melt on top of double boiler, over hot, not boiling, water. Chocolate should not exceed 110°F; remove from heat.

8 Pour one-fourth of the melted chocolate onto a smooth, clean Formica or marble surface. Work back and forth with a flexible metal spatula until opaque. Scrape back into the bowl of chocolate and mix until smooth. Continue in this manner until mixture is cooled to 80°F.

9 Return chocolate to double boiler and heat to 85°F.

10 Dip each ball in tempered chocolate and sprinkle ground almonds on top of each. Refrigerate until ready to serve.

Kitchen scale: A scale is useful for accurate measuring. Try to buy one with the conventional and metric weights. Keep it in a handy place to use whenever you need it.

Chocolate Truffles Framboise

Yields 20 truffles

8 oz.	semisweet chocolate
8 oz.	heavy cream
1 oz.	Raspberry brandy
12 oz.	semisweet chocolate for coating
2 oz.	Dutch process cocoa, sifted

1 *To mix the truffles*: In a clean, stainless steel bowl, over a double boiler, melt the 8 oz. of semisweet chocolate over hot, not boiling, water. Add the cream; heat together, whisking until smooth and the chocolate melts. Add the raspberry brandy.

2 Place in a bowl and refrigerate for 1 to 2 hours.

3 Using a pastry bag fitted with a no. 5 plain piping tip, fill the bag with the chilled mixture; pipe 1-inch balls onto a baking sheet lined with parchment.

4 Place in the freezer for 10 to 15 minutes till the balls are quite firm.

5 Roll each ball between your palms till smooth and round; return to the freezer.

6 *To prepare the coating*: Chop 12 oz. of semisweet chocolate; melt in a double boiler over hot, not boiling, water.

7 Using a fork, dip each ball in chocolate, covering them evenly. Shake off excess chocolate.

8 Roll each ball in sifted cocoa and transfer to a tray. Refrigerate until ready to use.

Chocolate Truffles White Chocolate Marzipan

Yields 20 truffles

8 oz.	marzipan (available in specialty shops)
1 oz.	Kirsch liqueur
12 oz.	white chocolate
4 oz.	powdered sugar, sifted

1 In a mixing bowl, combine the marzipan and Kirsch; using a wooden spoon, blend until smooth. Roll into 1-inch balls.

2 Melt the white chocolate on top of a double boiler over hot, not boiling, water, stirring continuously until melted.

3 Using a fork, dip each marzipan ball in melted chocolate and shake off excess; then roll in the sugar. Refrigerate until needed.

Petits Fours Chocolate

Yields 20 petits fours

½ recipe   Chocolate Spongecake (page 116)
            apricot jam

for GLAZE

6 oz.   bittersweet chocolate
6 oz.   heavy cream
1 oz.   sugar

for DECORATION

1 oz.   bittersweet chocolate

1 *To make the petits fours*: Cut cake into 1-inch round or square shapes.

2 Coat each piece lightly with apricot jam.

3 *For the glaze*: Chop chocolate finely; melt in a double boiler over hot, not boiling, water.

4 In a saucepan, heat the cream and sugar to the boiling point.

5 Whisk hot cream into the melted chocolate; cool for half an hour.

6 Using a fork, immerse each glazed piece of cake in the warm glaze and place on a wire rack. Cool for 10 to 15 minutes.

7 Melt 1 oz. bittersweet chocolate over hot, not boiling water.

8 Using a paper cone or pastry bag filled with no. 00 plain tip, draw lines of melted chocolate over each petits fours.

9 Using a small palette knife, loosen each cake from the rack and place onto a cake plate or serving platter. Refrigerate until needed.

German wines are often used as an apéritif wine as well as with dessert.

Boil: The liquid bubbles briskly (water boils at 212°F or 100°C).

Fondant

Yields 1 pound
- 1 lb. sugar
- 8 oz. water

1 Mix sugar and water in a saucepan and bring to a boil. Boil until the syrup reaches the soft ball stage (260°F).

2 Pour onto a cold stainless steel pan or a cold marble surface; work with a spatula until the syrup becomes white.

3 When cool, store in a covered plastic container.

4 Heat over a double boiler when needed. Leftover fondant can be stored again.

Petits Fours Baumkuchen

Yields 20 pieces

for SPONGE

7 oz.	unsalted butter, softened
1¾ oz.	cornstarch, sifted
5	egg yolks
1¾ oz.	sugar
5	egg whites
4¼ oz.	sugar
1¾ oz.	ground almonds
1¾ oz.	all-purpose flour

for GLAZE

8 oz.	Fondant (recipe follows)
	water
	chocolate, melted, for decoration

1 Whip the softened butter in a mixer; then add the cornstarch. Blend for about 5 minutes on medium speed until the mixture is very light in color.

2 In a separate bowl, whip the egg yolks and sugar until the mixture is stiff and has a pale lemon color.

3 In a separate bowl, whip the egg whites and sugar until soft peaks form.

4 Gently fold whipped egg yolks into the butter mixture; then fold in the egg white mixture; lastly, fold in the ground almonds and the flour.

5 Line a 9 × 11-inch baking sheet with parchment. Using a metal spatula, evenly spread one-fifth of the batter to all corners of the baking sheet.

6 Bake at 350°F for 5 to 6 minutes until golden. Cool for about 5 minutes.

7 Spread another one-fifth of the batter over the cooled layer, as evenly as possible. Bake until golden.

8 Proceed in this manner until all the batter is used up and 5 layers of Baumkuchen are achieved. Cool the cake on a rack.

9 Cut cake into 1-inch round or diamond shapes using a cutter.

10 Glaze with fondant.

11 Decorate, as desired, with melted chocolate.

Wine and Cheese

Why do people say "wine-and-cheese"? Are they really a good match?

In my opinion, the answer is yes. Let's look at some of their similarities. Wine is produced from different grape varieties and cheese from different types of milk (cow, goat, sheep, reindeer, buffalo, even yak). Climate, soil, and geography affect the finished results. Did you ever drink milk in the spring after the cows had munched through a field of new onions?

The processes of making wine and cheese both require the skills of dedicated craftsmen. Minute variations in the amount of fermentation (for wine) or the humidity of the curing room (for cheese) create unique products. Both can age and be consumed at various stages of their development. Many similar adjectives are used to describe wine and cheese: earthy, complex, smoky, fruity, and nutty are just a few. Their flavors vary from mild, to medium, to full-bodied.

How is cheese categorized and what are its characteristics?

Cheese is categorized into seven different families, and like all families there are similarities between its members.

1. *Fresh cheeses* are uncured and only one step from the milk stage. They are ready to eat while still very moist. Generally mildly flavored and rich with a light tang, they cannot be preserved for long. Some fresh cheeses are mascarpone and Ricotta (from Italy) and St. Yves, Boursin and Roulé (rolled with herbs, spices, or strawberry purée), all from France.

2. *Soft-ripened cheeses* are one of the most popular categories—often dubbed the Brie family for its most famous member. These cheeses get their remarkable taste from the way in which they are made. After the curds are formed, the cheese is salted lightly on the outside and sprayed with a white mould that ripens it into a golden, soft texture. Brie, Camembert, St. André, L'Explorateur, and Pont L'Evêque are a few of the many French soft-ripened cheeses. Limburger is from Germany; Liederkranz is from the United States.

3. *Semi-soft cheeses* are creamy and rich with velvety textures and aromas that range from mild to strong. Many of them were originated in the monasteries of the Middle Ages. St. Paulin, Port

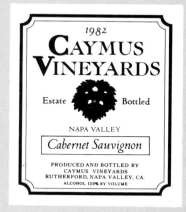

French soft-ripened cheeses are often referred to as single, double, and triple crèmes, which means that the butterfat content is 50, 60, and 75 percent, respectively. The higher the butterfat content, the richer and smoother the taste of the cheese will be.

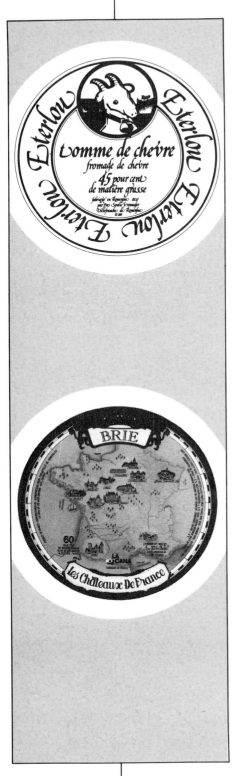

Salut, and Morbier are a few of this type from France. Bel Paese and Fontina d'Aosta are Italian cheeses. Others include: Gouda (Holland), Tilsit (Germany), Havarti (Denmark), and Sonoma Jack (United States).

4. *Chèvres* are goat cheeses, and since goats do not produce an abundance of milk, they are the world's most expensive. This cheese is coveted for its unique flavor—a hint of sharpness and acidity, a slightly peppery tang, and an earthy, nutty character. Goat cheeses are produced around the world and most often called by their shape rather than a brand name. Bucheron and Montrachet are the most widely available French chèvres. Feta cheese, which is made from sheep's milk, is from Greece.

5. *Blue-veined cheeses*, with their distinctive marbling and tangy flavor, which include more than sixty varieties, are the aristocrats of the cheese world. A properly aged blue cheese must have well-developed veins extending throughout its body to possess its special piquancy. Roquefort, Pipo Crème, Bleu de Bresse, Saga Bleu, Stilton, Gorgonzola, and Maytag Blue, are some of the world's big blues, coming from France, Denmark, England, Italy, and the United States.

6. *Semi-hard and hard cheeses* carry their most prominent family resemblance not so much in a common taste or aroma but rather in their firm textures. In this group are the famous mountain cheeses from France and Switzerland called the Gruyères. Excellent with sandwiches or to eat plain, they have complex, nutty flavors, including Emmentaler, Beaufort, Comté, and Cantal. From England are the Cheshires and cheddars; from Norway, Jarlsberg; from Holland, Edam. Italy's famous grating cheeses—Pecorino-Romano, Parmigiano-Reggiano, and Grana Padano—are also related to this family.

7. *Processed cheeses* are the stuff of school cafeterias. They comprise a majority of mass-consumed supermarket cheeses. America produces the bulk of the processed cheeses sold on its shores, but other countries produce them as well. Perhaps the kindest thing that can be said about these cheeses is that they keep remarkably well.

What are the three most popular types of cheeses served in restaurants?

Soft-ripened cheeses, semi-soft cheeses, and chèvres (goat cheeses) are most frequently seen on restaurant menus. In the soft-ripened family, Brie is the undisputed king, responsible for the growth of the specialty cheese market in the United States in the last ten years. The large pie-thick wheel is completely edible, including the outside white mould. Camembert is a smaller downy-white plump disk that must be kept whole until it is ripe. If it is cut too early, the ripening process is disturbed and the cheese never reaches perfect maturity. St. André, also from France, is the most popular triple-crème cheese sold in America. Its flavor is quite mild (made from vegetable rennet) and its texture melts in your mouth with a richness akin to fine ice cream. The triple-crème cheese L'Explorateur has a much more pungent flavor than St. André.

The Legend of Cheese

The origins of cheese date back to about 9,000 B.C. when animals were first domesticated. There are many legends about how cheese was first created and many countries claim the credit for it. Here's my version (with license taken for the sake of an interesting story, of course).

In ancient Sumeria, a travelling merchant prepared himself for the day's hot journey across the desert. In addition to his usual foodstuff, he filled his shoulder bag (made from the stomach of a calf) with fresh milk. Then off he went on his camel.

It was an arduous journey with very few rest stops. When at nightfall he planned to sup, he found to his dismay that the contents of his makeshift canteen had solidified: only a thin, sourish liquid remained, plus some solid, lumpy things. Not having much choice, he cut open his bag and consumed the transformed milk. Not bad, he mused. How'd I do that?

Of course, we know now that the rennet naturally present in the stomach lining of a suckling animal combined with the heat and agitation of the day's journey had separated the milk into curds and whey.

No doubt the enterprising Sumerian rushed home with his discovery and set up the first specialty cheese shop in the civilized world. But that's another story.

In the semi-soft category, Port Salut (Port of Salvation) cheese, which has an inedible orange rind, smooth texture, and mild flavor, was first created by Trappist monks in Brittany. From Italy comes Bel Paese, another cheese whose formula was handed down by priests. Doux de Montagne (Sweet of the Mountain) is a nutty-flavored cheese with small holes.

Chèvres have become enormously popular in the last ten years. All the variations available have the characteristic tangy flavor of goat's milk. You will most likely encounter two French chèvres in restaurants: Montrachet—a creamy log that may be dusted with vegetable ash, and Bucheron, an extra-creamy variation that is generally more acidic than Montrachet. Americans are producing some very high-quality goat cheeses, which are not as pungent as their French counterparts.

Make Way for the Gruyères

Long ago when the people of Gaul paid tribute to their kings and emperors, some of the levy was paid in gold and some in cheese. The princes sent their agents (the original IRS agents), who accomplished their fiscal goals so splendidly that they were given noble rank. This middle-management nobility took as their coat of arms the crane or *grue*—that large migratory bird known for its messy nests and habit of summering in the Alps.

From the word "grue" came "gruyer," which was known as the term for tax collector. It later evolved to "Gruyère," describing the cheeses or payments themselves. Many a medieval tax collector became extremely agile at dodging these huge (220-pound) cheeses as irate peasants decided to roll them down the mountains when the tax rate climbed too high.

A Nutritional Breakdown of Cheese

Cheese is rich in high-quality protein, containing significant amounts of all the amino acids, plus calcium and phosphorus. Because cheese is such a concentrated food, a small portion can provide a large part of your daily intake of protein. Since the fat in cheese slows digestion, you feel satisfied with a little bit.

When *during a meal should cheese be served?*

There is no right or wrong time to serve cheese. In Europe, a fresh, mild cheese is often served at breakfast; at lunch, with crusty bread; at night, after the salad and before dessert. In the United States, we frequently serve it at the cocktail hour, and cheese is also served as an appetizer in some restaurants (fried mozzarella sticks are quite popular). At Windows on the World, we sell a large number of cheeseboards for special banquets; at the Cellar in the Sky, cheese is a separate course.

How *should cheese be served?*

Cheese tastes best and shows its finest flavor at room temperature (68°F). Take it out of the refrigerator about 30 minutes before you plan to serve it. Only take out as much as you plan to use at one time; often, taking cheese out of the refrigerator hastens deterioration. Cheese should be cut according to its shape so that the rind is evenly distributed and it is easier to keep.

When serving a cheese course, choose at least three different types of contrasting flavors and shapes. Arrange them on a board with enough space for easy cutting with a separate knife for each cheese to prevent flavor transference. If you wish, decorate your platter with greens, small bunches of grapes, and strawberries. Offer crusty breads and crackers in a nearby basket.

Buying and Storing Cheese

The best advice for buying fresh, ready-to-eat cheese is finding a reputable cheese store. Select a specialty retailer rather than a supermarket chain. If you are buying a cheese for the first time, ask for a taste.

Cheese should never be stored in the bottom of your refrigerator. Never freeze it. Keep strong-flavored cheeses away from delicately flavored foods. It's a good idea to change the wrapping on a cheese each time after you take it out; this avoids contamination with airborne bacteria that hastens spoilage.

The most frequently asked question when it comes to selecting cheese is how to tell if it is ripe. This applies particularly to the whole wheels of soft-ripened cheeses. Your sense of touch is the most important factor. Hold the cheese between your thumb and forefingers. Gently press the top and bottom, starting from the outside and working your way towards the middle. Feel how the cheese "gives." If it seems much firmer towards the middle, the cheese is not yet ripe. Of course, some people prefer their cheeses on the young side, when flavors are milder.

How do you make a match of wine and cheese?

When matching wine and cheese, consider the flavor and body of each. In general, a full-bodied, full-flavored wine goes well with a similar type of cheese. High-acid cheeses go well with high-acid wines. Personal taste (as always) is the prime governing factor. At the Cellar in the Sky, we serve a full-bodied red wine with the cheese course, mainly due to the progression of wines served throughout the evening. However, there are many cheeses that go well with white and sparkling wines.

Can you suggest some well-matched cheeses and wines?

French L'Explorateur cheese with Champagne—the bubbles in the wine cleanse the palate after tasting this rich triple-crème cheese. A spicy Alsace Gewürztraminer would also go well. Try St. André with a California Sauvignon Blanc. The acidity of the wine contrasts nicely with the creamy texture of the cheese, yet neither overpowers the other. Also try a Pouilly-Fumé or Champagne with St. André.

Fresh cheeses, such as Boursin, Boursault, Rondelé and Roulé, complement Beaujolais and Beaujolais-Villages wines. Perfectly ripe Brie and Camembert harmonize with a Meursault from Burgundy, a California Chardonnay, or a light red Bordeaux. Chambolle-Musigny is a full-flavored Burgundy that has enough complexity to stand up to an earthy Pont L'Evêque, a washed-rind cheese from Normandy.

Goat cheeses, because of their high acidity, match well with high-acid white wines from the Loire Valley. Many French goat cheeses are produced in this area, and it's natural that Pouilly-Fumé and Sancerre complement them nicely. A Bourgogne, red Côte de Beaune-Villages, or California Pinot Noir are good choices if you prefer to serve a red wine.

Port Salut, which is often served at Windows on the World for banquets, matches well with a Rutherford Hill Merlot, Simi Cabernet Sauvignon, or light red Bordeaux. Fontina from Italy and Gruyère from France or Switzerland are chewy, nutty-flavored cheeses with a lot of taste. A Rhône Valley wine, such as Châteauneuf-du-Pape, will complement without overpowering those cheeses. Talleggio and Bel Paese, both from Italy, are creamy and smooth cheeses that should be served with a well-aged Chianti or Brunello. Brebis—a semi-soft sheep's milk cheese from France—can stand up to the intensity of an Italian Barolo with ease.

In matching blue cheeses with wines, there are two schools of thought. Roquefort and Sauternes are considered a classic match. The saltiness and bite of the cheese is tamed by the unctuous sweetness of the wine. English Stilton is served with Port in its homeland. I cannot recommend serving dry white wines with blue cheese—they have no chance of competing with their potent flavors. Instead, reach for the fullest red you can find—a wine from the Rhône Valley or the Piedmont region of Italy.

BROWN VEAL STOCK

Use as stock in brown veal sauces; reduce for a concentrate.

Yields 2 Quarts

4 oz.	vegetable oil
4 lbs.	veal bones, skins and end cuts, chopped into small pieces
4 oz.	carrot, chopped
6 oz.	leek, washed and chopped
4 oz.	celery, sliced
6 oz.	onion, chopped
2 oz.	tomato paste
10 oz.	dry white wine
4 qts.	water
6	bay leaves
1	fresh rosemary sprig
½	fresh thyme sprig
a few	parsley stems (optional)
a few	mushroom stems (optional)
½ oz.	salt

1 Heat a roasting pan or heavy skillet and add the oil, veal bones, and trimmings.

2 Place in a preheated oven and roast at 350°F for about 1 hour or until golden brown. Stir occasionally with a wooden spoon.

3 Add the carrot and leek. Continue roasting for 5 minutes; then add the celery and onion. Roast for another 5 minutes.

4 Remove from the oven and place on the burner. Skim off the excess fat. Add the tomato paste. Roast thoroughly, then deglaze with half of the wine. Reduce the liquid. Repeat the previous step with the remaining wine.

5 Pour in 1 quart of the water and bring to a boil, stirring until diluted. Transfer to a stockpot and add the remaining water. Bring to a boil and skim off the excess fat. Stir in all the herbs, parsley stems and mushrooms, if using, and the salt.

6 Simmer gently for about 1½ hours. Strain through a cheesecloth directly into another pot. Degrease the stock and reduce to the desired amount. Strain again and cool.

7 Refrigerate and use within 3 days; or freeze for up to 3 months.

Fresh Tomato Sauce

Serve this sauce with Hot Chicken Liver in Puff Pastry, or grilled veal, beef, pork or fish. It can be made in advance.

Serves 8

1 oz.	shallot, chopped
1 oz.	olive oil
2 oz.	tomato paste
1	garlic clove, finely chopped
8	ripe Beefsteak tomatoes, peeled, seeded, and chopped
12 oz.	White Veal Stock (page 31) or White Chicken Stock (page 77)
1 oz.	heavy cream
¼ oz.	parsley, chopped
¼ oz.	fresh basil, chopped
1	sprig thyme leaves
	salt
	white pepper, freshly ground

1 Sauté the shallot in olive oil, then add the tomato paste and garlic, stirring well. Add the peeled and chopped tomatoes.

2 Pour in the White Veal Stock and simmer for about 15 minutes.

3 Add the heavy cream and reduce to about 12 oz. of liquid or until the sauce thickens. Add the parsley, basil, and thyme. Season with salt and pepper.

WHITE FISH STOCK

This is the stock to use for white fish sauces or soups.

Yields 1 quart

2 lbs.	*fish bones from red snapper, sole, or flounder*
2 qts.	*cold water*
2 oz.	*shallot, peeled and chopped*
4 oz.	*leek, washed and sliced*
3 oz.	*celery, chopped*
2	*fresh mushrooms, chopped*
1	*fresh thyme sprig*
2	*bay leaves*
5	*white peppercorns*
½ oz.	*salt*
4 oz.	*dry white wine*

1   Clean the fish bones and cut in small pieces with a large knife. Rinse under cold water and drain.

2   Place bones in a 4-quart stockpot and pour in the water. Set pot over a low burner and slowly bring to the boiling point. Using a skimmer or small spoon, discard the fat and foam rising to the surface.

3   Add the vegetables, herbs, spices, and wine. Lower the heat and simmer gently for 30 minutes, or until reduced to 1 quart.

4   Dampen a double cheesecloth and drape it over a Chinese strainer. Set over a bowl. Strain the stock; discard the bones in the strainer. Cool the stock.

5   Store stock in the refrigerator to use within 4 days; or store in the freezer in 2-cup quantities for up to 3 months.

BEURRE BLANC

Serves 8

4 oz.	*shallot, chopped*
9 oz.	*dry white wine*
⅓ oz.	*white wine vinegar*
5 oz.	*White Fish Stock, (recipe above)*
18 oz.	*unsalted butter, softened, cut in pieces*
	salt to taste
	white pepper, freshly ground

1   In a saucepan, simmer the shallot in the wine, vinegar, and stock. Reduce the sauce until the liquid is nearly evaporated.

2   Add the softened butter, piece by piece, stirring constantly.

3   Season with salt and pepper. Strain through a fine Chinese strainer. Keep warm at about 140°F in a double boiler.

Never remove a covered pot from the stove when you cannot see the liquid. Uncover the pot, take off the lid, and then move the pot. Otherwise, you may easily burn yourself with the hot liquid.

Beurre blanc creates a different flavor when some Noilly Prat vermouth is added to the white wine. You can also add freshly chopped herbs such as basil, chervil, or tarragon as a finishing touch to the sauce. A large spoonful of fine caviar provides a flavorful touch.

BROWN LAMB STOCK

Yields 2 quarts

2 oz.	olive oil
4 lbs.	lamb bones and trimmings, cut into small pieces
3 oz.	carrot, diced
4 oz.	celery, diced
3 oz.	leek, diced
4 oz.	onion, diced
2 oz.	shallot
2	garlic cloves
2 oz.	tomato paste
6 oz.	fresh, overripe tomato
8 oz.	dry white wine
3 qts.	water
2	bay leaves
1	fresh rosemary sprig
2	fresh thyme sprigs
1	fresh mint sprig
6	white peppercorns
1	fresh tarragon sprig
	salt

1 Heat a roasting pan or heavy skillet and pour in the olive oil. Add the chopped bones and brown slightly.

2 Roast the bones in the pan in a preheated oven at 350°F for about 1 hour or until evenly browned.

3 Add the carrot and celery. Continue roasting for about 3 minutes; then add the leek, onion, shallot, and garlic.

4 Skim off the excess fat; add the tomato paste and tomato. Roast for a few minutes.

5 Remove from the oven and deglaze with the wine. Add 2 quarts of the cold water and bring to a boil. Skim off the excess fat.

6 Transfer the bones and liquid to a larger stockpot. Add the remaining water and the herbs and spices; bring to a boil.

7 Lower heat and simmer gently for about 2 hours, skimming off the excess fat occasionally.

8 Strain through a cheesecloth into a saucepan. Add the brown veal stock and reduce over low heat to the desired quantity. Cool and degrease the stock.

9 Refrigerate and use within 3 days or store in the freezer.

When making stocks, if the water evaporates, always add *cold* water (never warm). If the liquid evaporates too much, no doubt your burner is too high!

You can store any stock in the freezer to keep handy for sauces and soups. Skim off and discard all fat from the surface before freezing. Pour into 2-cup containers when the stock is cool. Plastic containers won't absorb the odors if stocks are poured in when cool.

Three-quart saucepan: Useful to make and to reduce sauces and to reduce stocks.

Five-quart stockpot: You can use a large stockpot to make smaller quantities, so it is better to have a large one.

BORDELAISE SAUCE

Yields 16 oz.

2 lbs.	beef and veal bones, finely chopped
2 oz.	vegetable oil
4 oz.	onion diced
3 oz.	carrot, diced
2 oz.	leek, diced
3 oz.	celery, diced
3 oz.	tomato paste
3 oz.	mushrooms
6 oz.	red Bordeaux wine
15	white peppercorns
2	bay leaves
	salt, as needed
2 qts.	Brown Veal Stock (page 153)
1 oz.	beef bone marrow, diced

1   In a heavy pan, roast the beef and veal bones in the oil at 350°F for 45 minutes to 1 hour. Add the diced vegetables and roast for 10 minutes.

2   Add the tomato paste and mushrooms; roast for 3 minutes. Deglaze with half of the wine. Continue roasting until liquid is reduced; then add the remaining wine and again reduce the liquid.

3   Stir in the Brown Veal Stock. Bring to a boil and skim off the fat and foam. Add the peppercorns, bay leaves and salt.

4   Cook slowly in the oven for about 2 hours, adding water, if necessary. Reduce to about half the original amount. Strain through cheesecloth into another saucepan.

5   Bring the sauce to a boil on a burner. Skim off the fat. Cook until the desired consistency; you should have at least 12 ounces of sauce remaining). (If the sauce is not thick enough, mix a teaspoon of cornstarch with a little red wine and add to the boiling sauce.)

6   Remove from heat. Add the bone marrow. Serve hot.

Degrease: When stock begins to boil, to skim off the fat and foam rising to the top, using a shallow spoon; or to remove the fat by spreading a heavy paper napkin over the stock or sauce and discarding the paper that absorbs the fat.

Index

Recipes are listed by category in italics.